Defensive Handgunning

A Treatise on Handgun Carry and Use

Glenn Rehberg

Defensive Handgunning

A Treatise on Handgun Carry and Use

All rights reserved. No part of this book may be reproduced or transmitted in any form by any electronic or mechanical means (including photocopying, recording, or information storage and retrieval systems) without written permission from the author, except for the inclusion of brief quotations in a review.

© 2007 by Glenn Rehberg
First edition, 2007

ISBN 1434810364

EAN-13 9781434810366

For Wilbur, whose leadership made it possible,

and

Paige, for supporting me without reservation.

"It is not best that we should all think alike;

it is a difference of opinion that makes horse races."

-Mark Twain

Table of Contents

WHY THE DEFENSIVE HANDGUN? 1
- WHISTLES, ALARMS, AND CELL PHONES 4
- PEPPER SPRAY AND STUN GUNS 5
- HANDGUNS 7

BASIC ELEMENTS OF HANDGUN USE 11
- STANCE 13
- GRIP 15
- SIGHT ALIGNMENT AND SIGHT PICTURE 19
- TRIGGER CONTROL 21
- PUTTING IT ALL TOGETHER 26
- CONCEPTUAL REVIEW 27

LOADING, RELOADING, AND MALFUNCTIONS 29
- ADMINISTRATIVE UNLOADING AND LOADING 30
- EMERGENCY RELOAD 32
- HANDGUN MALFUNCTIONS 38

CARRYING THE HANDGUN 45
- CARRY SYSTEM CONSIDERATIONS 47
- HOLSTER CARRY SYSTEMS 48
- HOLSTER-LESS SYSTEMS 54

DRAWING FROM A HOLSTER 57
- DRAWING AND MOVEMENT 60
- DRAWING FROM A HOLSTER 61

TACTICS 71
- SITUATIONAL AWARENESS 71

CONFRONTING A THREAT 73
TARGET AND TARGET AREAS 75
COVER AND CONCEALMENT 77
TRAVERSING LEFT AND RIGHT 81
MOVEMENT 83
IS THE THREAT OVER? 88
MULTIPLE ASSAILANTS 89
CLOSE-QUARTER DISTANCES 91
SHOOTING WITH ONE HAND 94
LOW LIGHT ENVIRONMENTS 100
FIGHTING IN AND AROUND VEHICLES 103

MINDSET 107
MINDSET EXERCISES 110
MENTAL REHEARSAL 113
TRAINING ADJUNCTS 116

POST-SHOOTING ACTIONS 119
IMMEDIATE TACTICS 119
SCENE ACTIONS 122

SELECTING A DEFENSIVE HANDGUN 127
HANDGUN MODIFICATIONS 136
SELECTING AMMUNITION 138

GLOSSARY 143

BIBLIOGRAPHY 147

Disclaimer

This book is designed to provide information on the proper use of handguns in life-threatening encounters. It is written with the understanding that the author is not engaged in rendering legal services or advice. If such services or advice are needed, the services of a competent lawyer should be sought.

Throughout the book, the handgun user is responsible for following the four rules of firearm safety:

1. *Treat every gun as if it is loaded.* Some reputable instructors teach, "All guns are always loaded," to simplify and emphasize this rule. When a firearm is transferred, the recipient is responsible for personally inspecting the firearm to ensure it is unloaded. After inspection, continue handling every firearm as if it is loaded. Many deaths have occurred with "unloaded" guns.

2. *Never point the gun at anything you are not prepared to destroy.* Even after verifying a weapon is unloaded, keep it pointed in a direction that will safely stop any bullet fired.

3. *Keep your finger outside the trigger guard until you want the gun to fire.* Placing your finger inside the trigger guard must not occur until you want the weapon to discharge.

4. *Be sure of your target and what is beyond.* Be certain you have positively identified your target and gunfire doesn't endanger an unintended target.

About the Author

Glenn Rehberg is a Sergeant on a small Wisconsin police department. As the agency's training coordinator, he trains department personnel in all areas related to use-of-force. Besides being certified by the Wisconsin Department of Justice as an instructor in Firearms, Defense and Arrest Tactics, and Vehicle Contacts, he has received advanced training through the Lethal Force Institute, SureFire Institute, Strategos International, National Tactical Officers Association, Simunition Inc., Glock Inc., Colt Defense L.L.C., Federal Bureau of Investigation, Midwest Training Group, InSights Training Center, Defensive Edge Training & Consulting, L.M.S. Defense, and E.A.G. Tactical. This is his first book.

Foreword

By Greg "Sully" Sullivan

Given the wealth of information available today on handguns, one can easily become overwhelmed and be misinformed. As someone with years of real-life experience, I know first hand how challenging it can be to maintain current knowledge of the various types of weapons and how to properly use them.

Glenn Rehberg's book "Defensive Handgunning: A Treatise on Handgun Carry and Use" provides one of the most comprehensive and well-organized books on Defensive Handgun that I have seen.

Glenn's practical experience with handguns, coupled with his vast knowledge of the mindset, gleaned from countless hours training and carrying a handgun, provides the reader with a solid basis of learning to use a handgun defensively. This book covers not only how to shoot a gun, but also how to properly carry and draw a handgun, as well as proper storing, cleaning and ammunition. Glenn takes the best of the best information for mindset and gives a clear understanding of the importance of mindset.

Greg "Sully" Sullivan is an active duty law-enforcement officer with 20+ years on the streets. He applies his real-world knowledge to his training and the products he's developed, such as the SLR15 Rifle and Sully Stock.

Acknowledgements

This book is an attempt to describe a systematic, comprehensive approach to fighting with a handgun. None of the components of this system are personal inventions. Instead, the system is a collection of inter-operable ideas and techniques gathered from an array of instructors that pass one important test—being effective and practical on the street.

I must express my appreciation for the feedback and comments provided by Tom, Kris, Carrie, and Irv. This book wouldn't be what it is without them.

I would like to especially thank Ken Good (Strategos International) for his outstanding training on low-light confrontations, the OODA Loop, and breathing; John Holschen (InSights Training Center) for his pointers on grip; Randy Revling (BCSD/NWTC) for his emphasis on thorough programming of basic competencies; Andy Kemp and Bob Houzenga (Midwest Training Group) for their work on draw and long-range pistol shooting; Charlie Warren (Wisconsin State Patrol) for his use-of-force instruction; and Greg "Sully" Sullivan (Defensive Edge Training & Consulting) for his knowledge of movement, fighting around vehicles, and invaluable personal support.

Introduction

I have been fortunate to train with many excellent instructors. Each instructor taught principles, techniques, and methods intended to obtain maximum effectiveness from a sidearm.

Occasionally, however, I found that techniques taught by the instructor clashed with other principles or techniques taught by that same instructor. Or, techniques taught by one instructor conflicted with techniques and principles put forward by other instructors. Though a particular technique worked in isolation, it conflicted with the development of a cohesive, principled, comprehensive, interconnected system.

"Hick's Law" worsens a confusing situation. Hick's Law states the reaction time to a stimulus lengthens as the number of possible responses increases. In other words, practicing different techniques that accomplish the same thing may be counterproductive, because the practitioner spends time navigating choices rather than reacting with one effective, trained technique.

Finally, a review of books on handgun self-defense revealed well-intentioned authors with little practical experience, and/or books that spent far too much time on esoteric topics while glossing over critical basic skills.

I set out to write a book incorporating the best techniques into a system that had no inherent contradictions, while utilizing the minimum number of non-standard responses. When confronted with a deadly threat, the user could react with a trained, universal technique instead of engaging in ineffective analysis and decision-making under stress.

Whether I have succeeded is left to the reader.

Why the Defensive Handgun?

In a perfect society no one would need to carry a weapon. Police would be unnecessary, and crime—especially violent crime—would be non-existent. Unfortunately it is all too evident that our society hasn't yet achieved that condition. The daily news is filled with stories of armed robberies, spousal abuse, child abductions, and rapes. Violent crime rates have risen the last three years, particularly in medium-size and Midwestern cities, after enjoying a 40-year low. Even with today's relatively "low" crime rate, a violent crime occurs every 22 seconds and the number of violent crime victims increases daily. A forcible rape occurs every 5 minutes, and an aggravated assault occurs every 36 seconds.[1] 1.4 million violent crimes occurred in 2006 alone.

---

[1] Federal Bureau of Investigation, <u>Crime in the United States 2006: Uniform Crime Reports</u>.

Chapter One

Some of us may go through life without experiencing the effects of violent crime. Even in today's era of relatively low crime rates, however, an unacceptably large number of people will be victimized. Recent statistics show a yearly violent-crime victimization rate of 17/1000 for females age 12 and over.[2] Although a relatively low violent crime rate is good news, a cursory look at the U.S.D.O.J. Bureau of Justice Statistics webpage shows America is far from safe. Many factors play into the likelihood of experiencing violent crime, but no location anywhere in the United States is a safe haven from predatory criminals. The difference in per-capita crime rates between large "dangerous" cities and small "safe" rural towns is not as great as stereotypically portrayed. An individual playing the odds about whether he or she will be victimized risks losing the bet.

In this environment of potential victimization, individuals are left to make their own choices regarding personal security. There are different options to choose from, ranging from denial of the problem to debilitating paranoia. At one extreme, believing "it can't happen to me" is too often proven wrong. On the other hand, people who feel trapped in their homes to avoid victimization are prevented from living the life they could be experiencing. Individuals are left to decide a response to these dangers. Within the spectrum of possible responses lies the carry and use of defensive instruments, possibly including a handgun.

Many books provide suggestions on how to prevent becoming the victim of a criminal assault. This is frequently followed by a description of

---

[2] U.S. Department of Justice, Bureau of Justice Statistics, <u>Violent Victimization Rates by Gender, 1973-2004</u>, identifying homicide, rape, [armed] robbery, and assault.

Why the Defensive Handgun?

makeshift tools and non-deadly weapons that *might* be considered, if defensive tactics are discussed at all. The carry and use of a defensive handgun is seldom mentioned; when it is, it is usually discouraged.

Fortunately, data collected by the U.S. Department of Justice has been studied to determine victim injury rates based on what, if any, self-defense method was used. According to that study, victims utilizing guns to defend themselves were *least* likely to be injured—even less likely than people who did not resist at all.[3] This data has also been analyzed to determine who is more likely to be injured. Women were more likely to be injured in an attack than men.[4]

An examination of self-defense literature finds tidbits of good advice often incorrectly touted as solutions to the problem. For example, a single woman venturing out alone at night faces increased chances of assault. Many have therefore promoted the adage, "Don't go out at night by yourself." Women, particularly, receive this advice. However, advising women to stay inside after dark is unrealistic, sexist, and unacceptable. It's unrealistic, because following such a regimen would limit her employment and lifestyle. Are women prohibited from buying milk at the corner convenience store, or responding to after-hour family emergencies? Beyond being unrealistic, it is inherently sexist, demanding that women follow behavior patterns forced upon them by young men—the most common class

---

[3] Journal of Quantitative Criminology, "Victim Resistance and Offender Weapon Effects in Robbery", Gary Kleck and Miriam A. DeLone, Vol. 9, No. 1, March, 1993; and Targeting Guns: Firearms and Their Control, Gary Kleck, Aldine de Gruyter, 1997.

[4] U.S. Department of Justice, Bureau of Justice Statistics, Injuries from Violent Crime 1992-1998, 06/01 NCJ 168633.

Chapter One

of criminal assailants. If late hours at the office are needed to climb the corporate ladder, are women to be kept from advancement? Avoiding unnecessary trips through dark high-crime areas is certainly good advice for everyone. But is the woman who cannot heed this advice left without an alternative to submitting to assault?

Having acknowledged one bit of good advice—that *everyone* is best served avoiding high-crime areas when possible—and knowing that such a suggestion cannot set an intractable boundary on one's life, other commonly-offered advice should be examined. What about the makeshift tools and non-deadly weapons commonly recommended?

Whistles, Alarms, and Cell Phones

Although whistles and personal alarms are touted as a solution, physical and psychological limitations may reduce their usefulness. Whistles and alarms are useful when drawing attention to your predicament would result in assistance. However, there are locations where the repeated shrieking of a whistle is only a signal to shut the curtains and avoid looking outside. In 1964, bystanders ignored Kitty Genovese's screams for help as she was attacked, raped, and murdered over the course of a half hour. No one called police until after Kitty was dead. The "Bystander Effect," the phenomenon of not receiving help when in obvious danger within view of a number of people, has subsequently been studied in depth. Other unfortunate examples include Deletha Word in 1995 and James Bulger, a two-year-old, in 1993.

Why the Defensive Handgun?

The use of a whistle to summon aid has other inherent limitations. What if no one is nearby to hear it, such as in a late-night parking garage, an isolated home, or a broken-down vehicle on the highway?

Whistles and personal alarms are one method of attracting attention to one's plight. Cellular phones are another method of summoning aid. Cellular phones are a recommended tool and a significant adjunct to personal security, but also have important limitations. Coverage in remote areas is spotty or non-existent. They are battery-dependent, so may not work when needed. Until GPS-enhanced phones become common, the user must know their precise location at all times for help to arrive. The caller must be able to speak; a hand clamped over the caller's mouth will prevent use of the cell phone. Also, cell phones require a significant amount of time. The potential victim must dial, communicate the problem, provide their address, and then wait for help to arrive. Depending on police response times, this could be a long wait. Finally, the caller must remain immobile to ensure help will find them. If the caller flees or is dragged away, rescuers may not find them.

Whistles, personal alarms, and cell phones are useful tools that have a place in the defensive toolkit. Their effectiveness lies in discouraging or dissuading an attack, or in summoning aid after an attack has already been completed. However, they do nothing to prevent a determined assailant from completing their assault.

Pepper Spray and Stun Guns

Non-lethal tools such as pepper spray and stun guns occupy a very useful position in personal defense. In the right circumstances they might

Chapter One

interrupt or end many criminal acts. Even simple physical resistance may deter some assailants or allow the potential victim to escape with minimal injuries. However, the potential effectiveness and reliability of these defenses must be examined against the level of threat present.

As an example, pepper spray is a useful tool against a single, unarmed assailant who hasn't previously experienced being sprayed. Used properly and with a modicum of good fortune, the attack is foiled, the assailant is marked with UV-dye for the police, no one suffers long-term ill, and the intended victim escapes. This is a happy ending.

There are drawbacks to the use of aerosol sprays, however. In enclosed areas or where the wind direction is wrong, the defender might receive as much of the spray as the attacker. The limited range of aerosol sprays may not provide the time and distance necessary to escape from a group of attackers—and use of multiple assailants is a common tactic for criminals to better their odds. If the victim doesn't successfully escape the group of attackers, the victim will face the assailants they sprayed—and the assailants will likely be very, very angry about it. Furthermore, some experienced fighters, especially those who have been sprayed before, may treat the spray as a mere inconvenience and fight through or ignore its effects. Finally, people under the influence of alcohol or drugs are commonly less affected by the spray.

Stun guns[5] suffer even more limitations than aerosol sprays. They demand the defender spend long seconds within contact range of the

---

[5] Wisconsin laws will sometimes be cited for the benefit of Wisconsin residents. Electric weapons are illegal in Wisconsin, Wis. Stat. 941.295.

assailant—time during which the defender is within range of the attacker's fists, hands, knife, boots, etc. Bringing the stun gun into contact with the attacker may be difficult or undesirable, especially if the assailant is larger, more powerful, or has faster reflexes. A Taser™ may allow non-contact use, but the defender will generally have only one cartridge and no time to reload should the prongs miss or prove ineffective. Finally, assuming any electric device works, the effect wears off quickly when the electricity stops, leaving the assailant free to pursue the defender. And no electronic weapon is useful against multiple attackers.

Handguns

Many self-defense writers hesitate to recommend the use of force to counter an assault. However, the use of justifiable force against assailants has prevented or ended many attacks. When faced by an attacker who threatens death or serious injury, the defender is left with few defensive options that bear a reasonable chance of success.

A handgun gives its user a defensive ability unrelated to size, stature, gender, or handicap. A handgun is nothing if not an empowering agent. A famous nineteenth century quote embodies that premise: *God made all Men, Samuel Colt made them equal.* Consider the following situations.

- A woman attacked by a gang of four men
- An elderly man assaulted by a young, fit criminal
- Anyone confronted by a criminal carrying even a simple deadly weapon like a baseball bat

Notice that in none of the above scenarios does the victim face a criminal armed with a knife or a gun. Even so, each of the victims faces the potential

Chapter One

danger of death or great bodily harm.[6] A woman confronted by four men bent on gang rape faces poor odds even if she has years of training in unarmed self-defense. What, besides a handgun, can provide that woman with the ability to thwart the attack? What will give an elderly or infirm person the ability to resist and flee a fit assailant? How else can even a reasonably fit individual overcome the advantage that relatively poor, makeshift weapons—like a baseball bat—give to a single criminal willing to use them?

It is important to understand, however, that a handgun is no panacea against crime. Like a fire extinguisher, a handgun is a specialized tool. Within its design parameters, nothing else will perform its task as ably or as effectively. Nothing else enables a defender, regardless of size, gender, or age, the ability to thwart the life-threatening attack of a criminal. If the defender must use deadly force, only a handgun is small enough and convenient enough to be handy when needed.

However, when deadly force isn't appropriate a handgun isn't the tool for the job. An extreme example of this is road rage, where people have waved guns at other drivers for committing traffic offenses. An assailant who doesn't present the danger of death or great bodily harm doesn't warrant the threat or use of deadly force. A handgun's usefulness is limited to unexpected situations where deadly force is potentially appropriate. If the attack could have been foreseen, the defender wouldn't be there, and if

---

[6] "'Great bodily harm' means bodily injury which creates a substantial risk of death, or which causes serious permanent disfigurement, or which causes a permanent or protracted loss or impairment of the function of any bodily member or organ or other serious bodily injury." Wis. Stat. 939.22(14).

deadly force isn't warranted, a handgun serves no useful purpose. Within those constraints, however, handguns serve admirably.

Because of its limited utility, a handgun is most useful when incorporated into a larger system of situational awareness and defensive tactics.

This book will not delve into self-defense laws beyond stating that prior to using deadly force, the defender must be under imminent threat of death or great bodily harm and have no reasonable alternative to the use of deadly force. Laws vary from state to state, and readers are responsible for knowing the laws affecting them. Several excellent resources are listed in the bibliography for further study of this critical component.

This book is for readers who have decided to learn to use a handgun for self-defense. The rest of the book shows how to effectively employ a handgun while maximizing the user's survivability. Chapters discuss how to carry, conceal, and use a defensive handgun in an integrated system.

Chapter One

Basic Elements of Handgun Use

Unlike many other books about handguns, this one begins with a discussion of the critical skills necessary to put bullets into the target. Pointedly, it does *not* begin with a summary of different handgun types and actions, the advantages and disadvantages of each, and how to select a handgun. Starting with equipment gives undue weight and importance to the hardware chosen and de-emphasizes the importance of the user's skills, tactics, and mindset. The brand and type of handgun chosen is much less important than the defender's ability to effectively operate that firearm. The equipment used has much less effect on an encounter's outcome than the defender's tactics and mindset. Good equipment is a valuable aid, but because it is less important, it will be discussed in the last chapter.

Chapter Two

It is easy to understand why many people give equipment more attention than it deserves. As a physical object, equipment can be easily purchased, measured, and tested. As a concrete entity it can be readily compared against other pieces of equipment. A handgun can be judged based on size, capacity, rust-resistance, or any number of other factors. Articles in gun magazines provide excellent examples of this over-emphasis on equipment: "9mm versus .45—Which is Better?", or, "Is the Revolver Still a Viable Defense Gun?", or, "We Test Remchester's Newest .45." Far fewer articles discuss tactics or training, and articles on mindset are practically non-existent.

Skills, tactics, and mindset are much more important than the equipment used, but receive much less attention. They receive less attention because they are not as easily acquired as a piece of equipment. It takes time and effort to become a competent handgun shooter but it only requires cash to buy a pistol. Maintaining a handgun requires infrequent service but keeping one's skills sharp requires regular practice. Equipment is the least important factor, but the easiest and most pain-free to acquire.

However, the effectiveness of any handgun is determined by the shooter's ability to put bullets into the intended target. Inability to hit the target endangers anyone beyond the attacker and wastes the defender's limited, precious time. Fortunately, proper operation of a handgun is well within the grasp of anyone with normal coordination and dexterity. The largest obstacle to learning is usually not physical, but mental—deciding to actually learn to shoot, and then dedicating the practice time and resources to do so.

Basic Elements

There are four components involved in shooting a handgun accurately: stance, grip, sight alignment/sight picture, and trigger control. Each of these will be examined individually.

Stance

Stance is the body positioning used to control the handgun. Stance consists of the positioning of the shooter's feet, pelvis, torso, head, and arms, and the interaction of these components. Ideally, a good stance provides balance, flexibility, and the ability to immediately employ a wide variety of defensive tactics. An effective stance serves as a basic platform for movement, weapon control, hands-on fighting, etc. Because gunfights are a fluid event, shooters will vary from a "textbook" stance during an actual shooting encounter. But the training stance adopted should be versatile and functional, as it serves as a foundation for learning.

Different stances have been touted by proponents claiming benefits unique to their system. Most stances have advantages in some areas and weaknesses in others. The goal is a practical stance that allows the defender to shoot as accurately and effectively as possible, while providing the flexibility and adaptability to employ any needed tactic. In a tumultuous fight for one's life, it will be difficult to shoot from a "perfect" stance. Therefore, the acid test is whether the stance can be employed dynamically in a fight, or whether it requires standing "just so" in order to perform the "correct" method of supporting the handgun.

The stance will vary depending on the shooter's physical build. The basic underlying concept is to adopt a stance that maximizes flexibility and mobility. The lower body, from the belt down, will work separately from the

Chapter Two

upper body. The lower body carries the upper body around while the upper body operates, aims, and fires the handgun. Each half of the body functions independently while shooting, though both are critical to success. Massad Ayoob has likened the upper body to a tank turret. The turret rotates independently of the chassis, while the chassis transports and stabilizes the turret, buffering it from bumps and uneven ground.

Begin by standing with feet slightly wider than shoulder-width apart, with the strong-side foot slightly behind the lead foot and the weight on the balls of the feet, not the heels. Slightly flex the knees to keep the body poised for movement, to absorb energy, and to allow quick movement in response to changing situations. Lean forward from the bottom of the rib cage, positioning the shoulders in front of the hips, as if pushing or shoving someone away or leaning over a counter. The goal is an aggressive forward posture that absorbs recoil energy into the main mass of the body.

Take both arms and push them forward as far as possible, locking the elbows. This will form an isosceles triangle between the arms and chest. The head may naturally drop down slightly between somewhat hunched shoulders, but should not be brought down so far that

Basic stance.

Basic Elements

breathing is impaired. Rather, the gun should be brought up to the level of the head. The overall posture is similar to what many people naturally adopt in a fight. This is an advantage, as trying to deprogram one's natural stance when confronting danger is counterproductive.

Grip

Grip is a key component of shooting, as it comprises the interface between the defender and the handgun. A poor grip will result in inability to properly control the handgun.

The two hands are referred to as the "strong" hand and the "reaction" hand. For a right-handed individual, the right hand is the "strong" hand while the left hand is the "reaction" hand.[7]

Wrap the strong hand around the handgun so it is as high as possible on the grip. No light should be visible between the gun's tang and

High grasp on grip.

---

[7] The term "weak hand" is not used because it subconsciously influences the behavior of that hand. A shooter who refers to their "weak" hand subconsciously programs that hand to be weak.

Chapter Two

the web of the hand between thumb and forefinger. Ideally a bunch of flesh may be jammed up there, forced into the tang by the high grip. The middle finger of the strong hand should be snug against the bottom of the trigger guard. If using a revolver, position the hand as high on the grip as possible while avoiding contact with the hammer.

Grip the gun so tightly that the gun almost begins to tremble. Even a firmer grip, where the gun begins to shake, won't degrade accuracy in a self-defense setting. Although this "crush grip" isn't used by target-shooting competitors, it nicely replicates how hard the gun will be gripped by a defender in fear of being killed. During a life-or-death struggle, it's unlikely the defender will grip the gun any less firmly than possible. By programming a firm grip, the shooter is conditioning herself to the environment and reactions they are most likely to experience under stress.

Except when the user actually wants bullets coming out of the barrel, the trigger finger should extend parallel to the handgun's frame above the trigger guard. The index finger should not be inside or alongside the trigger guard. Trigger-finger discipline is a key difference between a competent gun handler and a dangerous neophyte.

When the first pad of the trigger finger is eventually placed on the trigger, the handgun should be naturally in-line with the bones of the

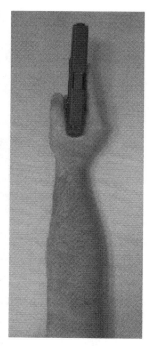

Gun in-line with arm.

strong arm. If the gun must be rotated in the hand towards the trigger finger

Basic Elements

for the first pad to be centered, the shooter is compensating for a handgun grip that is too large. The shooter should change to smaller grips (or use a gun with a smaller grip) so it properly fits the hand.

After a high crush grip is established and the gun is verified to be in-line with the strong arm, the other hand enters the picture. Despite what is seen on TV or in movies, it is much better to shoot with two hands than one when the situation allows it. Two-hand shooting provides increased weapon control and better accuracy.

While holding the handgun in the strong hand, observe the handgun grip. Most likely there is surface exposed between the fingertips of the strong hand and the base of the thumb. Take the heel of the reaction hand and firmly grind it into the exposed surface, as high on the grip as possible. Lift the strong thumb off the grip face to allow this high hand placement. After the reaction hand is in place, wrap the strong thumb over the reaction hand at about 45 degrees.

Rotate the reaction hand fingers down while leaving the base of the reaction hand high on the grip. This leaves the reaction thumb resting on the frame of the handgun, parallel to the

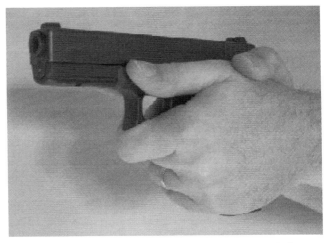

Reaction hand placed as high as possible on gun, with fingers pointing down at about 45 degrees. "Ayoob Wedge" shown.

17

Chapter Two

barrel, pointing at the target. Rotating the reaction hand as far forward as possible places the base of the thumb in-line with the arm and wrist bones, forming a flat surface. This may feel awkward initially. But it significantly reduces muzzle flip when the gun is fired.

Wrap the fingers of the reaction hand around the front of the grip, interlocking the fingers so the reaction fingers fall in the grooves made by the strong fingers. This prevents the reaction fingers from sliding off the strong hand when they become slippery from sweat or blood. If the reaction fingers are already in the grooves, they cannot slide off the strong fingers. The gun should be gripped *at least* as tightly with the reaction hand as by the strong hand.

If the base of the reaction hand is placed as high as possible on the side of the gun grip, the reaction fingers will point about 45 degrees down. To further lock the gun into the grip, utilize the Ayoob "Wedge."[8] Place the reaction hand's middle finger against the trigger guard, and then wrap the index finger above that. If the shooter's hand size and finger length allows it, this wedge effect will stabilize the gun by forcefully levering it into the strong hand.

The combination of a braced, flat surface of the reaction hand's thumb, wrist, and arm, combined with a strong grip by both hands, significantly reduces muzzle flip and helps prevent shooting with an unlocked wrist. This results in reduced gun movement during recoil, allowing faster, more accurate shooting.

---

[8] Massad Ayoob, <u>Stressfire Vol. I</u>, p. 32.

Basic Elements

Sight Alignment and Sight Picture

Having established stance and grip, the next step is properly aligning the gun with the target. There are two components to this: sight alignment and sight picture.

Sight alignment consists of aligning the handgun's sights. With a few unusual exceptions, every handgun is equipped with a front and rear sight mounted on the top of the barrel or slide. The sights indicate where the fired bullet will strike—when properly aligned, at the tip of the front sight.

When the sights are properly aligned the front post will be centered in the rear sight notch and the tip of the front sight will be level with the top of the rear sight, like this:

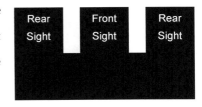

If the sights have dots or other markings on them, concentrate on the edges of the sights. Dots or other markings are not as precise and are intended to aid low-light shooting, discussed later.

Sight picture consists of focusing on the tip of the aligned front sight and placing it on the desired target. Various factors come into play, including the eye dominance of the shooter and the inability of human eyes to focus on objects at different distances at the same time.

Just as most people are either left- or right-handed, most people have an eye that is dominant. Usually, but not always, the dominant eye is on the strong side of the body, i.e., a right-handed person is usually right-eye dominant. To test this, make a circle with your thumb and forefinger. With both eyes open, focus on an object on the other side of the room, put the

Chapter Two

circle around the object, and bring the circle closer to the eye until it's clear what eye is looking through the circle. That eye is dominant.

The sights are brought in front of the dominant eye to obtain the sight picture. However, the eye cannot simultaneously focus on all three objects involved—target, front sight, and rear sight. To shoot accurately, it is necessary to focus on the front sight. The rear sight will be somewhat fuzzy and the target will be out of focus. This is normal and provides the best accuracy possible.

Both eyes open; gun in front of dominant eye.

Focusing on the target is common under stress. However, that focus makes accurate sight alignment impossible, causing shots to scatter. This significantly reduces accuracy and reduces the defender's effectiveness.

Shoot with both eyes open. While practicing, many people believe it is easier to achieve proper sight alignment and sight picture if they close the non-dominant eye. With practice, closing one eye is usually not necessary. Under stress the brain naturally wants to see what's endangering it. Human instinct is to keep both eyes open in a life-threatening defensive encounter.

Closing one eye may work well on the target range, but is counter-intuitive in close-range defensive engagements.

Trigger Control

The most important factor in achieving rapid, accurate shot placement is proper trigger control. Some instructors emphasize the importance of the front sight until students hear it in their sleep. Admittedly, aligning the front sight with the target is very important to achieve hits. However, if the shooter doesn't use good trigger control, it hardly matters where the front sight is placed—the bullets won't hit there anyway. Poor trigger control results in shots being scattered away from their aiming point, while proper trigger control ensures the bullets strike where they were aimed.

Good trigger control causes the gun to fire without disturbing the existing sight picture. The challenge in achieving this goal is twofold: first, pressing a trigger weighing four to twelve pounds on a two-pound gun without moving the weapon; and second, doing so rapidly while under stress. Trigger control is a skill that can be achieved through proper training reinforced with periodic practice.

To perform a proper press, the trigger finger must be isolated from the other fingers, and the trigger finger must not rub on the handgun as it performs the trigger press.

Isolating the trigger finger is necessary to prevent other fingers from working sympathetically. It is natural for all fingers to work cooperatively. As an example, when a hand picks up an object, all of the fingers curl around the object, not just a few of them. This cooperation becomes problematic when one finger is asked to individually perform a critical task under stress.

Chapter Two

If other fingers tighten or loosen when the trigger is pressed, the handgun will shift in the grip, causing inaccuracy.

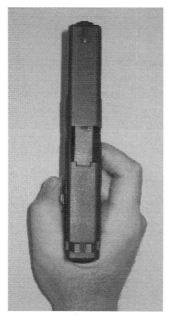

Finger doesn't touch frame when finger is on the trigger.

Utilizing the aforementioned crush grip helps isolate the trigger finger. Because the rest of the fingers are already gripping as hard as they are able, they cannot exert additional force when the trigger finger moves. Indeed, because of the relatively high exertion by the other fingers, the index finger's effort may seem light in comparison.

The other precursor to a proper trigger pull is preventing the trigger finger from rubbing on the frame during the pull. If the trigger finger pushes on the frame as the trigger finger moves, the gun will shift slightly, again reducing accuracy. To prevent this, examine the entire trigger finger while its first pad is centered on the trigger. Looked at from above, the finger should be a mildly curved "C," with light visible between the finger and the handgun's frame. The trigger finger should not lie flat against the frame. If it is flat against the frame, the best solution is to buy smaller grips or a smaller gun. When using a gun that is too large, some shooters are forced to rotate the gun in their grip to shorten the trigger reach. This takes the gun out-of-line with their arm and reduces the effectiveness of their stance. These shooters should use a gun with a smaller grip rather than compromise their ability to shoot the gun accurately.

Basic Elements

After the trigger finger is isolated and doesn't lie on the frame, a proper trigger press can be performed. With the first pad of the finger centered on the trigger, gradually apply pressure directly backwards into the trigger. Applying pressure in any direction other than straight backwards will cause inaccuracy. Continue to gradually increase the pressure until the gun fires.

This application of pressure must be performed *smoothly* and *steadily*. The shooter must never feel as if they are hurrying or accelerating the trigger pull. Press slowly so the exact moment the gun will fire cannot be predicted. As the shooter becomes more practiced, the pace at which pressure is applied can be gradually increased, compressing the time period during which the surprise discharge will occur. Even when the shooter has progressed to shooting extremely rapidly, the actual press is still not "hurried"; instead, it's performed during a very narrow window of time.

Not hurrying the trigger press is a key principle. If the shooter tries to make the gun go off *right now*, the trigger finger naturally convulses or "snatches" at the trigger. This sudden, forceful jerk will cause serious inaccuracy. Snatching the trigger is a very common problem. When done without other shooting errors, it will pull shots low.

With practice it is possible to shoot very quickly without snatching at the trigger. Picture a slow, steady application of trigger pressure. Then, visualize that same trigger press occurring over a somewhat shorter time period. Perform the same unhurried press over shorter and shorter time periods until the presses occur very quickly, yet still unhurriedly. There is a significant difference between the "rapid yet unhurried" press and the "snatch." To avoid programming destructive habits, the shooter must only shoot as fast as they are able to perform a smooth trigger press. It bears

Chapter Two

repeating: this takes practice to master, yet only a few bad repetitions to instill bad habits. Progress slowly.

When a pistol fires, the trigger should be held to the rear. If the shooter wishes to fire another shot immediately, the trigger should then be released just far enough to reset the trigger mechanism. In other words, the trigger is released just far enough to allow the trigger to be pressed again. The distance will vary, but the shooter can detect this by the "click" of the reset. Releasing the trigger beyond the sear reset point wastes time and motion. Even worse is taking the finger off the trigger between uninterrupted shots. By only releasing the trigger to the sear reset, the shooter increases speed and reduces the trigger movement necessary to fire the next shot.

If the shooter does not want to fire another shot immediately, the trigger finger must come off the trigger and be placed above the trigger guard alongside the frame.

Dry-firing

The best practice for trigger control is dry-firing. Begin with an empty gun. Physically and visually check to ensure the gun is unloaded: no magazine present, no cartridge in the chamber, and no ammunition in the same room. Check again, and yet again. This triple-check must be a religious, inviolable rule. Most gun accidents occur with a gun the shooter thought was unloaded.

After ensuring the gun is unloaded, aim at a solid backstop that would safely stop any bullet accidentally fired. Slowly apply trigger pressure until you hear the gun's firing pin "click." The gun's front sight should remain absolutely motionless when the firing pin falls. If the gun muzzle twitches or moves suddenly, the trigger was not pressed smoothly. Dry-firing will not harm any quality handgun[9] and should be performed thousands of times to program the proper press into muscle memory.

Anticipating recoil

Another commonly encountered shooting error is anticipating recoil. When fired, a handgun will "jump" slightly in the hand. This recoil is explained by Newton's third law of motion: for every action there is an equal and opposite reaction. Because the gun is propelling a bullet downrange, the gun recoils in the opposite direction of the bullet. Combined with the leverage exerted by the shooter's hand, placed below the barrel axis, this will cause the handgun to recoil backwards and the muzzle to flip up. Except in unusually light or powerful handguns, this recoil will not be painful. It can be disconcerting, however, to have an inanimate object jumping around in the hand.

With a proper stance and grip, the amount of gun movement during recoil will be minimal. The gun's muzzle will twitch upwards slightly and then return to the target almost instantaneously. Accept that movement as permissible. To further minimize this movement, solidify the grip and use an aggressive stance with proper weight distribution. Do not physically fight this movement during recoil.

Many shooters anticipate this movement and try to counteract it. It's natural, but incorrect, to fight this movement and try to keep the gun pointed exactly at the target during recoil. When making this error, the shooter

---

[9] Dry-firing will not harm any quality centerfire handgun. It *can* harm .17 and .22 rimfire handguns; refer to the handgun's owner manual.

pushes the gun down when it's believed the gun will fire. This downward push, or anticipation, is sometimes visible even before the gun fires. It seriously impedes accuracy, throwing shots very low.

The best fix for this problem is twofold. First, mentally accept that the gun will jump somewhat when it is fired. Second, give it mental permission to do so. Anticipation is best cured through the use of ball-and-dummy drills.

"Ball" refers to practice ammunition, and "dummy" refers to inert or replica cartridges that do not fire. Ball-and-dummy drills are done during live fire. The shooter or his/her coach loads the gun with one or more inert "dummy" rounds mixed among live rounds. The shooter begins firing, and when the shooter attempts to "fire" a dummy round, any anticipation will be visible as the gun dips downwards. By seeing and feeling this movement, the shooter is forced to acknowledge his or her anticipation. The remedy to anticipation is a large amount of dry-firing combined with ball-and-dummy drills (beginning with a high percentage of dummies versus live rounds).

Putting It All Together

It's crucial that the shooter begin slowly, striving for correct stance, grip, sight alignment and picture, and trigger press. Shooting a handgun is a physical skill similar to golf, riding a bicycle, or skiing. A beginning golfer won't hit 200-yard drives. Attempting to do so will only slow their learning and instill bad habits. Similarly, a new shooter will not shoot rapidly and accurately their first few times at the range. It is crucial to shoot accurately and master the basics *before* trying to gain speed.

Basic Elements

Conceptual Review

The most important principle in this book is this: ***you cannot miss fast enough to win.*** Only hits can be counted on to win a defensive encounter. Firing a gun does not force an attacker to stop their assault. Only a sufficient number of bullet <u>hits</u> will force an attacker to stop. To get these hits as fast as possible, the shooter must often slow down and concentrate on basic skills. "Slow is smooth; smooth is fast."

The second principle of the system is that, while under stress, the user will perform what they've practiced most, or most recently. This is shown by any number of people who practice a fine motor skill and then use it under stress, such as football players, musicians, pilots, and soldiers. The key is practicing the skill properly and consistently, in the same manner. A person who practices five different methods of performing a task must take time to decide which of the methods to employ, whereas a person who has practiced one perfected method has no decision tree and simply executes the task.[10]

Finally, the last criteria guiding this system's development is that techniques must function under the adrenaline dump many defenders will experience. In a life-threatening encounter the body reacts by engaging its "fight-or-flight" response. This primitive response dumps a large amount of epinephrine, or adrenalin, into the body, which allows the defender to run faster and hit harder. It has other effects—small muscles have less dexterity and feeling; tunnel vision and time distortion are common; thinking may become difficult. Thus, simple techniques are generally preferred to more

---

[10] Hick's Law

Chapter Two

complicated techniques; techniques benefiting from strength are preferred to those requiring dexterity, and guiding concepts are emphasized over detailed "to-do" lists.

Loading, Reloading, and Malfunctions

The first step in handling any firearm is to determine whether it is loaded or unloaded. When receiving a handgun from another person, immediately examine it to determine whether it is loaded. *Another person's examination must never be trusted.* It is not disrespectful to repeat their exam; instead, it is an acknowledgement of the potential lethality of the handgun, and the acceptance of that responsibility by the new bearer.

When examining the firearm, follow all the rules of firearm safety. The weapon is not properly checked unless the examiner visually and physically inspects each component. It is not enough to look at the inspection points to determine if the firearm is loaded—the user must physically put their fingers where the ammunition would be if the gun is loaded. This tactile inspection is a second check that encourages the user to spend the time necessary for a thorough exam.

Chapter Three

Administrative Unloading and Loading

The person handling a firearm is responsible for ensuring it is unloaded. To safely examine a gun, all ammunition must be removed from the inspection site. For example, if a firearm will be examined at a range's firing point, all ammunition should be kept at a different firing point to prevent any possibility of inserting ammunition into the gun during the inspection.

The method used to determine whether a gun is unloaded is dependent on the type of handgun—revolver or semiautomatic pistol. Each inspection method includes both physical and visual components.

For revolvers, open the cylinder by pressing or pushing on the cylinder release latch and pushing the cylinder to the left from the frame. Inspect each chamber in the cylinder by physically touching each empty chamber hole and visually looking through every chamber. If the gun is unloaded, no rounds will be visible. If cartridges are present, press the ejector rod to remove the cartridges from the cylinder, and repeat the inspection.

Pistols have a two-step process. Begin by removing the magazine and physically and visually checking the magazine's feed lips for ammunition. Set the magazine aside, where it cannot be accidentally retrieved and inserted into the pistol. Even after the magazine is removed, a cartridge may remain in the firing chamber. Pull back the slide and lock it open. Do *not* place a hand over the ejection port in an attempt to catch any round that might be ejected. There have been incidents where ejectors have struck cartridge primers, detonating the round outside the chamber and causing serious hand injuries. After the slide is locked open, visually examine the chamber and insert a finger through the ejection port to physically examine the chamber.

Loading, Reloading, and Malfunctions

Note: It is **essential** that the correct sequence be used when inspecting a semiautomatic handgun. Remove the magazine *then* inspect the chamber. If the order is reversed with a loaded magazine, a live cartridge will remain in the firing chamber.

After the examination of the firearm has been completed and the user wishes to load the firearm, the following steps should be taken. Begin by stating to anyone present that all inspection, practice, dry-firing, etc. has ended. Even if no one else is in the room, this verbal warning focuses attention on the fact that the firearm is about to become a dedicated lethal instrument. Retrieve the ammunition from its separate storage location. Then follow the "Emergency Reload" steps below, beginning at the point where the gun is empty and the magazine, if applicable, has been removed.

After loading the handgun, it must be put into the proper status or "condition." If the handgun is equipped with a safety, the safety is applied; if the handgun has a decocking lever, the gun is decocked. A pistol's magazine may be topped-off by removing the magazine, inserting another round to replace the one just chambered, and firmly re-inserting the magazine into the grip.

Finally, immediately place the handgun into its safe storage location, i.e., a carry holster or lock box. The handgun must not lie around unsecured. Immediately securing the handgun helps prevent negligent discharges. There have been occasions where a weapon was loaded but not immediately placed in its storage location. Being distracted, the user "dry-fired" the now-loaded weapon, sending an actual bullet downrange.

Chapter Three

Emergency Reload

While defending one's life, everyone would agree it's important to reload an empty gun as quickly as possible. Most everyone would agree that making themselves harder to attack would be beneficial at this point—particularly if firing the now-empty gun hasn't stopped the attack yet. However, most handgun users fail to practice in a manner that programs the correct response for a life-threatening encounter. Consistent practice of the desired performance results in performing as practiced. *Perfect practice makes perfect.*

Begin by recognizing the gun is empty. The slide of a semiautomatic will be locked open, while a revolver will "click" instead of fire. Move completely behind cover to prevent being shot while holding an empty gun. (If practicing at a range where movement is impractical, take a step sideways in the shooting booth to simulate movement to cover.)

Emergency Reload--Pistol

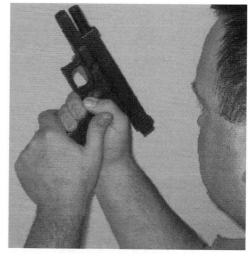

Gun brought up to face; magazine beginning to be forcefully stripped from pistol.

Begin by bringing the handgun closer to your face instead of performing the reload in an extended "firing" position. This provides greater dexterity and leaves the gun in your peripheral vision while looking towards the threat. Keeping the gun at face height encourages heads-up observation during the reload.

Loading, Reloading, and Malfunctions

Push in the magazine catch button (if right handed, use the right thumb; if left handed, use the trigger finger) and strip the magazine out of the magazine well with the reaction hand. The reaction hand grasps the base of the empty magazine while on its way to the spare magazine. This will result in the empty magazine being flung forcefully downwards. Some people worry this method may damage their magazine. Instead, they prefer to pluck out the empty magazine and place it gently on the shooting bench or in a pocket before reaching for the next magazine. While gentle on equipment, pampering the magazine trains a technique that is only useful as long as defensive gunfights are not under time pressure, have shooting benches nearby, and where shooter concerns about damaging a $25 magazine are more important than rapidly reloading empty guns.

Other people counter that their magazines drop free without assistance, so it is unnecessary to forcefully strip them from the pistol.

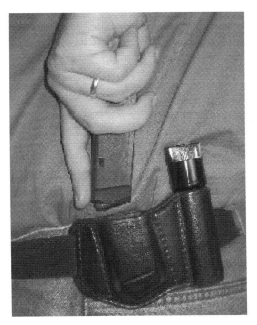

Reaction hand grasps magazine with index finger pointed to feed lips.

They are partially correct—some pistols' magazines are designed to drop free. However, if the magazine becomes dirty with the intrusion of sand or dirt, or the magazine sticks for one isolated incident, reloading becomes much more complex. On the other hand, always forcefully stripping the magazine will ensure that any

Chapter Three

magazine-fed pistol can be quickly prepared for a fresh, fully-loaded magazine, even if the gun is dirty or a malfunction is present.

After the empty magazine has been removed, a full magazine must be brought to the gun. This magazine is normally kept on the reaction side of the body, with the bullets facing towards the front center "belt buckle" area.

In this method, the reaction hand grasps the base of the magazine with the index finger on the front, pointing towards the feed lips. The magazine is withdrawn from the holder and rotated so the feed lips face up, with the index finger pointing the way to the magazine well.

Index finger points way to magazine well during reload.

The magazine is inserted into the grip and pushed home very firmly. It is not eased into place, but seated with a firm smack. A very common malfunction happens when the shooter fails to fully seat the magazine, resulting in only one round firing before the gun stops feeding new ammunition. This malfunction can be eliminated with proper handling of the magazine during the reload.

The pistol's slide is then closed. On most pistols the easiest method is to activate the slide release. Using the strong-hand thumb to do this is

34

Loading, Reloading, and Malfunctions

preferred, because this accommodates both one-hand and two-hand shooting methods. Use of the reaction-hand thumb works well for people with smaller hands, but does not promote universal methodology when shooting with only one hand. In addition, use of the slide release avoids interference with slide-mounted safeties and works on almost all semiautomatic pistols. After releasing the slide, the reaction hand is returned to the grip.

A few guns, however, require a different method of releasing the slide. Some guns, like the Glock™ and Smith & Wesson's™ M&P, are equipped with a small slide lock that was not intended to be used as a slide release lever. Other guns, such as the SigSauer™ P22x series, position the slide release in a position that some find difficult to reach with the strong-side thumb.

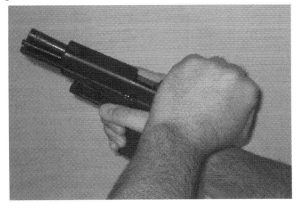

Releasing slide using overhand grip.

Shooters using these guns should use an overhand grip over the rear of the slide. Pull the slide completely to the rear with the reaction hand, again being careful to keep the hand behind the ejection port. When the slide has been pulled back as far back as possible, the reaction hand continues to the rear while releasing the slide. This prevents "riding" the slide forward and helps ensure proper feeding of the cartridge. By compressing the spring as far as possible, maximum force is available to feed the next cartridge and lock the slide shut.

Although the overhand slide release works well, it is not the preferred technique for a couple of reasons. Proponents of the overhand release

Chapter Three

believe it is a gross motor skill and therefore less susceptible to degradation under stress. However, swiping the slide release is less of a fine motor skill than pressing the trigger; the thumb can operate under stress. Furthermore, using the thumb to release the slide is a universal technique; it works whether the reaction hand is available, or whether the reaction hand is disabled from injury.

One universal constant is that the slide is allowed to slam forward to feed a round into the chamber. It must *not* be eased forward. The pistol was designed to operate at full speed. Rapid slide movement promotes positive cartridge feeding, while slow operating speeds, or "easing" the slide forward, will frequently cause a misfeed or a failure of the slide to lock closed.

Emergency Reload--Revolver

Bring the handgun closer to your face so it is in your peripheral vision while looking towards the threat. Thumb the cylinder release while sliding the reaction hand fingers around to the right side of the cylinder. With the left hand's fingers, press the cylinder to the left and point the revolver upwards. Smack the ejection rod with the palm of the reaction

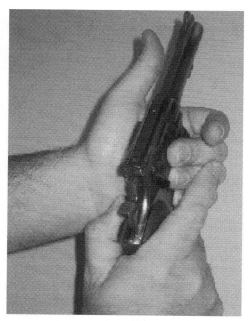

Cylinder pushed open from right.

Loading, Reloading, and Malfunctions

hand, allowing gravity and the ejector star to force the brass out of the cylinder. (A forceful strike will clear cartridges from revolvers whose ejector rod is not long enough to clear empty cartridges with a slow press.[11])

After the brass has been ejected, point the revolver towards the ground and secure it by cupping the cylinder in the left hand with the index and middle fingers straddling the ejector rod. Meanwhile, the right hand retrieves the speedloader or cartridges and places them into the cylinder, allowing gravity to assist. When the cartridges are fully seated, grasp the grip with the strong hand and close the cylinder with the reaction hand, allowing the speedloader to

Forcefully ejecting brass.

Inserting speedloader cartridges into cylinder.

---

[11] Smith & Wesson "J"-frame revolvers are one example.

37

Chapter Three

fall away.

Handgun Malfunctions

Any defensive handgun must be tested for reliability before it can be trusted. Every gun manufacturer has, at times, produced items that were defective, and the time to discover the problem is not during a life-threatening encounter. Before being relied upon, the handgun should digest at least 200 rounds of the chosen defensive ammunition without any functioning problem whatsoever. (Selection of defensive ammunition is discussed in Chapter 9.)

Some individuals complain that 200 rounds of premium defensive ammunition are too expensive to be used for this purpose. Instead, these people might run a single gun-load through the gun to test it. Others don't test their defensive ammunition at all, gambling that because it's premium ammunition, it should work without any problem.

This failure to thoroughly test the compatibility of a chosen gun and defensive load is a grave mistake. A quality handgun combined with quality ammunition *should* function flawlessly, but there are instances where tolerance stacking can cause unreliability. (For example, I purchased a Kahr™ PM9 pistol that wouldn't reliably feed any Speer's Gold Dot™ ammunition. This was an excellent gun that wouldn't reliably function with superb ammunition. I solved this by using a different defensive load—the PM9 functioned flawlessly with Winchester's Ranger™ ammunition.)

During the 200-round test the handgun should be fired with both hands, right hand only, left hand only, and from unconventional shooting positions. If any malfunction occurs, the problem must be diagnosed and fixed, or the

Loading, Reloading, and Malfunctions

test repeated with a different defensive load until 100 percent reliability is achieved. Any malfunction within the 200 rounds is a sign that the handgun/ammunition combination is not sufficiently reliable for defensive use.

Even after firing 200 rounds of the chosen defensive ammunition without any problem, no mechanical object is completely reliable. Malfunctions can be caused by dirt, faulty ammunition, improper operation, worn or broken parts, etc. The user must know how to fix or "clear" a malfunction as quickly as possible in order to make the handgun operable again.

The user should practice simple techniques that fix the malfunction, regardless of its cause. These techniques must be utilized during all training sessions to ingrain them as a reflexive response. Never call "time-out" to figure out what went wrong with the gun. No assailant is going to wait for the defender to diagnose the problem. Practice fixing the problem immediately! After the malfunction has been fixed and the shooting has been completed, the user can try to replicate the malfunction to allow diagnosis and repair.

Though increasingly uncommon, some instructors still teach diagnosing the specific malfunction and then performing the most-correct clearing process. Although the ability to diagnose the cause of a malfunction shows understanding of the handgun's cycle of operation, it has no place in a fighting system. Under severe stress diagnosis is impractical, time-consuming, and inappropriate. Instead, immediately clear the malfunction following the described process.

Chapter Three

Pistol Malfunctions

Many pistol malfunctions are caused by magazine issues, such as bent feed lips or the user's failure to fully seat the magazine.

As soon as some sort of malfunction is realized, the user should immediately move behind cover (if they're not already there). Without further diagnosis, perform the "phase one" clearing drill described below. If a "phase one" drill doesn't fix the problem, perform the "phase two" without any further analysis. If a phase two clear doesn't fix the problem, the gun isn't fixable in the field and the defender must formulate a new plan.

The "phase one" clear is done immediately upon recognizing any malfunction. The shooter smartly taps the base of the magazine with the base of the reaction hand, firmly seating the magazine in the gun. Then the shooter racks the slide sharply to the rear while rolling the pistol clockwise towards the ejection port. The reaction hand continues rearward when the slide reaches maximum rearward travel, releasing the slide to chamber another round. The gun is now, in theory, ready for use. This process is sometimes referred to as the "tap-rack-roll," "tap-rack-bang," or "tap-rack-assess" process.

A "phase one" clear fixes the most common reasons a pistol malfunctions. A magazine that is not fully seated frequently causes pistols to fail to feed ammunition into the chamber. The "tap" seats the magazine, the "rack" feeds a new cartridge, and the "rack/roll" should remove any defective or spent cartridge that might be present or failed to fully eject.

Some shooters—particularly self-taught shooters—tend to skip the "tap" in the clearing process. These shooters have enough experience to recognize and diagnose one possible problem—a round failing to feed or fire—but

Loading, Reloading, and Malfunctions

have not programmed *all* of the corrective action necessary to fix the potential cause. Thus, they rack the slide in an attempt to chamber a round, but haven't fixed the root problem—an unseated magazine. The purpose of a standard clearing methodology is to make diagnosis unnecessary, but *all* steps must *always be performed in order* to program the correct response in an emergency.

If the pistol doesn't fire after performing a "phase one" clear, a "phase two" malfunction clearing is performed. Lock back the slide using the slide lock, strip out the magazine in the pistol, rack the slide forcefully at least three times, insert a fresh magazine, and rack the slide to chamber a round. This is the "lock-rip-rack-rack-rack-reload" drill.

A "phase two" clear should fix any malfunction that can be fixed without tools or spare parts. Initially locking back the slide allows easier removal of the magazine when a feeding failure or faulty magazine caused the malfunction. Removing the magazine gets rid of a possibly damaged, empty, or faulty magazine. Repeatedly racking the slide gives the extractor multiple attempts to remove a cartridge that might have failed to extract from the chamber. Reloading with a new magazine provides an undamaged magazine full of cartridges.

Revolver Malfunctions

Revolvers are somewhat less likely to malfunction because of ammunition or improper shooting technique. However, they are still a machine subject to wear and mechanical failures, and can still malfunction.

If a malfunction occurs, the revolver user should move to cover. Fully release the trigger and attempt to pull it again. If the trigger is frozen or the

Chapter Three

cylinder doesn't revolve, the user will have to diagnose the cause of the malfunction.

Failure to fire, without other apparent problems (the trigger moves normally, the hammer rises and falls, and the cylinder rotates) is likely a result of all ammunition having been fired. Perform an emergency reload and reassess the situation. If a reload doesn't fix the failure to fire, the revolver has a loose or broken part or the ammunition is faulty. Neither is likely to be fixed in the field.

Another common malfunction is a case trapped under the extractor star while reloading. This might be caused by failing to hold the revolver vertical when ejecting cases, or by "pumping" the ejector rod. The stuck case must be pried out using some sort of tool.

Case trapped under extractor star.

Finally, failure of the cylinder to rotate when the trigger is pressed can be caused by bullets trapped between the forcing cone and the cylinder. This can be caused by a "squib" (underpowered) load, or by bullets being pulled from the case by inertia in heavy-recoiling guns.[12] The only emergency fix is to force the bullet back into the case, using a rod

---

[12] For example, Smith & Wesson warns users of their Scandium and Titanium revolvers to check for bullets becoming unseated during recoil. S&W Owner's Manual Rev100906.

Loading, Reloading, and Malfunctions

that fits within the barrel. This is definitely *not* what a person in the middle of a gunfight wants to do, and emphasizes the importance of using good ammunition that has been thoroughly tested before carrying it for self-defense.

Chapter Three

Carrying the Handgun

Once the user has learned to safely operate a handgun and understands the legal requirements for the use of deadly force, they may be ready to begin carrying the handgun. After all, a handgun is useless if it's not available when needed.

A well-known quote summarizes the balancing act presented by carrying a pistol: "A handgun should be comforting, not comfortable."[13] In other words, it's bothersome and uncomfortable to carry a handgun around all the time. According to one study, people who report carrying a gun for self-defense only carry about 40 percent of the time.[14] A significant

---

[13] Clint Smith, Thunder Ranch.

[14] Kleck, Gary. <u>Targeting Guns: Firearms and Their Control</u>, Aldine de Gruyter, 1997, p. 206.

Chapter Four

contributing factor is this: carrying a concealed handgun is inconvenient. It's heavy. It requires specific clothing to conceal and demands constant awareness to keep it secure. It can affect the user's activities. The carrier cannot remove covering garments if it's too warm, must dodge hugs from casual acquaintances, cannot consume alcohol, etc. After encountering these limitations, many users only carry a handgun when going somewhere they perceive as potentially dangerous. Because it is unlikely they will need a gun that day, some permit holders come to the conclusion there is little need for routine carry of a handgun.

The statistical likelihood that a gun won't be needed today persuades some permit holders to carry infrequently, or not at all. However, that sort of statistical analysis is inherently flawed for multiple reasons. Statistically, most police officers will go their entire career without shooting at a criminal. Based on that, a similar argument could be made that police don't need firearms! There are two reasons why the statistical approach to being armed is inappropriate whether applied to police officers or concealed-carry permit holders.

Having seen all strata of society, police prepare for worst-case scenarios. While it is statistically unlikely a firearm will be fired during any particular shift, police are aware of the consequences of needing a gun and not having it. The extreme penalty for not having a firearm when it is needed outweighs the relatively low likelihood the handgun will be used.

Furthermore, the assailant dictates when a handgun is needed, not the victim. Criminals routinely try to take advantage of increased numbers, speed, and/or strength to overwhelm their victims. If the assailant believes they have the advantage, the defender will not have time to retrieve a firearm from elsewhere. The analogy of the fire extinguisher from Chapter One is apt. Fire extinguishers are rarely needed, yet universally recommended. When it is needed, it's needed immediately, in the immediate vicinity, and nothing else will substitute as well.

Carry System Considerations

Finding a "carry system" that works is a process full of balancing acts. The user must weigh competing factors:

- the need for quick access vs. the importance of concealment
- the handgun's accuracy and power vs. the size of the weapon
- the handgun's "shootability" versus its weight

An initial consideration might be the method by which the handgun will be carried. Will the handgun be in a belt holster? Will an off-body system like a purse be used? Or will the handgun be concealed nearby in a glove box or dresser drawer?

There are many different ways to carry a gun, and manufacturers are hard at work designing something "new and improved" all the time. Rather than risk an untried, unproven system, most handgun users are better off beginning with a system that has proven its usefulness in the past. Such methods include:

- Belt holster
- Ankle holster
- Shoulder holster
- Pocket holster
- Abdominal pack (fanny pack)

Chapter Four

- Belly-band/tucked-in holsters
- Purse or day-planner
- Rapid-access methods (dresser drawer, glove box, etc.)

Generally, a system works well if it completely conceals the handgun, allows a quick draw, carries the gun securely, and can be reached by either hand. Unfortunately, no method invented thus far is perfect, and each method has advantages and disadvantages.

Systems based around the use of an on-body holster are generally the fastest and most secure. On-body holster systems are recommended over off-body or holsterless systems because the handgun is readily available and is easier to secure from loss or theft. Off-body methods such as a purse or day-planner are convenient, but must be weighed against the risk of theft or loss. Misplacing a day-planner or being the victim of a purse-snatching becomes quite hair-raising when a weapon is involved.

Holster Carry Systems

Belt Holsters

There are many different kinds of belt holsters. All of them share the foundation of a belt that carries and stabilizes the holster on the hip. Depending on its design, the holster may be placed almost anywhere on the belt. The most common locations of belt holsters are "strong-side," "cross-draw," and "small-of-back." In addition, strong-side holsters may be either outside the waistband ("OWB") or inside the waistband ("IWB").

Carrying the Handgun

Belt holsters are one of the most common and effective ways for males to carry a handgun. Men's fashions typically include a belt, and are less form-fitting than female fashions.

For women, current fashions are generally form-fitting, making concealment difficult. Many women find their higher waist line and curved hips result in the handgun's grip being forced into their floating ribs. Holsters designed specifically for females tend to ride lower and tilt the gun outwards to avoid this problem, but exacerbate the form-fitting clothing issue.

Belt holsters work best when combined with a belt specifically designed for handgun carry. Double-thickness belts are sometimes used to prevent "holster flop," although quality single-thickness belts can also serve well. Common widths for gun belts range from 1¼-inch to 1¾-inch, with some manufacturers producing belts that fashionably narrow near the buckle. No dress belt found in a typical clothing store will be stiff enough to properly support the weight of a handgun.

Of the various kinds of belt holsters, an outside-the-waistband holster worn on the strong side hip just behind the seam of the pants is most common. When combined with a jacket, sweatshirt, or other concealing garment, the handgun is unobtrusive yet readily

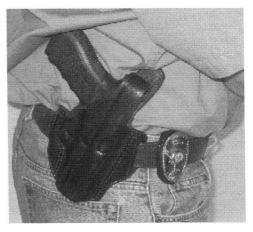

DelFatti belt holster with thumb snap.

Chapter Four

available.

For increased concealment, many people use an inside-the-waistband holster. Although some people find this requires pants with a waist size an inch or so larger, the handgun is hidden inside the pants with only the grip exposed above the belt. This allows better concealment, and the pants aid in stabilizing the gun.

Kramer inside-the-waistband holster.

Cross-draw holsters are worn towards the front of the body on the side opposite the strong hand, with the grip of the gun pointed towards the midline. Although some people prefer this method, it is generally less concealable than a strong-side holster. It also points the handgun grip towards an assailant, potentially making it easier to grab. Females may find cross-draw holsters more comfortable than strong-side holsters designed for men.

Some holsters angle the gun almost horizontally and are designed to be worn in the small of the back. These holsters are *not* recommended. Besides carrying the handgun in a location that's hard to defend from a gun grab, they offer an insignificant concealment advantage. Worst of all, a fall could result in spinal injury.

Finally, "Mexican" carry consists of tucking a pistol into the waistband without the use of a holster. This is *not* recommended and is *potentially*

Carrying the Handgun

unsafe. A quality holster protects the trigger from inadvertent movement and prevents the gun from falling out of the pants. Mexican carry has neither of these protections.

Ankle Holsters

Ankle holsters are designed to carry the handgun on the inside ankle of the leg opposite the strong hand. In other words, an ankle holster for a right-handed shooter would carry the gun on the inside of the left ankle. Ankle holsters work best for small, light handguns. They are slower to draw from and immobilize the user during the draw. However, ankle holsters are convenient to use while seated or in a car.

Ankle holsters require wide pants legs. Pants that are too narrow will exhibit a noticeable bulge and the pants will tend to ride up, revealing the gun. However, boot-cut jeans or wide-leg dress pants work well.

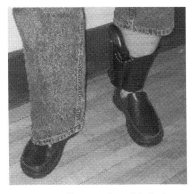
Renegade ankle holster.

Some users find the one-sided weight uncomfortable and disconcerting, while others aren't troubled. Ankle holsters are an excellent method for carrying a back-up handgun. Because they are slower to draw from and immobilize the user during the draw, they should be approached with strong reservations for carry of a primary handgun.

Shoulder Holsters

Shoulder holsters allow wearing a handgun whenever a jacket may be worn. Available in both horizontal and vertical styles, they carry the

Chapter Four

firearm underneath the armpit opposite the strong hand. Spare ammunition might be carried underneath the strong-side armpit, and some holsters use straps that attach the system to the waistband to reduce swaying.

Shoulder holsters can be uncomfortable depending on the user's physique. Some people find their arms are forced uncomfortably away from their side. Long-barreled handguns tend to protrude when worn horizontally, and vertical holsters may take up as much waistband space as a belt holster. Drawing from a shoulder holster requires care to prevent "sweeping" or pointing the gun at the user's body. These holsters are commonly prohibited in training classes because of draw "sweep."

Some women find shoulder holsters a viable option when compared to uncomfortable belt holsters.

Pocket Holsters

Slipping a small gun into a pocket is a fast, discreet, and convenient method of carrying a handgun. Pocket holsters aid this method of carry by keeping lint or debris off the gun, breaking up the outline of the firearm in the pocket, and keeping the handgun properly oriented for a fast draw. Pocket carry requires a small firearm. About the only

Uncle Mike's pocket holster.

Carrying the Handgun

disadvantages are the inability to carry a larger gun, and the difficulty drawing from a front pants pocket while seated or with the opposite hand.

Abdominal Packs

Abdominal packs or "fanny packs" are a convenient method of carrying a handgun while dressed informally. However, many people believe these packs "scream" gun, especially large black packs. Another significant disadvantage is the necessity of two hands to perform a rapid draw.

Fanny packs should be specifically designed to carry a firearm. Generic fanny packs that don't include an integral holster may allow the handgun to discharge by inadvertent bumping of the trigger. Nothing except the handgun should be carried

Bianchi fanny pack with integral holster.

in the holster compartment to prevent interference with the handgun or the draw.

Tucked-in Holsters

There are a few holsters that allow carrying a handgun near the waistline while wearing a tucked-in shirt. These holsters can be divided

DeSantis "belly band."

Chapter Four

into "belly bands" and "workman"-type holsters. "Belly bands" are wide elastic straps that are worn underneath the shirt. Besides carrying guns, they allow discreet carry of cash, identification, or traveler's checks. "Workman"-style holsters are belt holsters with a special slot to allow the shirt to be tucked-in between the holster and the belt.

For either method, thin guns with short barrels work best to prevent a noticeable bulge. The draw is slower and usually requires two hands, but concealment is excellent.

Holster-less Systems

Systems that don't use an on-body holster have advantages and limitations. At times they may provide increased convenience, but they usually provide less security and are not always accessible.

Purse or Day-planner

As an off-body holster system, this method combines the advantages of a holster with the convenience of off-body carry. To carry safely in this manner, it's important to use a purse or day-planner designed for the purpose. Purpose-made purses have a compartment designed solely for safely carrying a handgun. Containing a holster securely held by sewing or Velcro, these compartments combine stability and rapid access. On the other hand, carrying a handgun in a container not designed to prevent movement of the trigger is very dangerous. But, when used with a purse designed to safely carry a handgun, convenience and safety can be achieved.

Carrying the Handgun

There are several disadvantages to off-body carry. The handgun might not be accessible when it is needed—it's easy to walk away from a day-planner or purse set on a desk. Drawing the handgun requires two hands, when one hand might be busy keeping an attacker at arm's length. Purpose-built carriers are expensive. Galco purses, for example, are the best of the type, but cost several hundred dollars. Finally, security is a concern. For example, a successful purse-snatcher now has a weapon. Theft is a possibility any time the carrier is set down.

Rapid-access Methods

Dresser drawers, vehicle glove boxes, and quick-access safes are all methods to store a handgun within reach while not requiring on-body carry. These methods share the disadvantages of all off-body systems—possible unavailability when needed—but dispose of the inconvenience of actually carrying a handgun.

Security and availability remain the biggest concerns with these methods. Security is a particular concern for firearms left in a vehicle or in an unlocked location accessible by children or unauthorized users. Anyone considering "stashing" a firearm in a convenient location should carefully consider the security aspects and significant potential hazards.[15] Furthermore, when the user

Quick-access safe

---

[15] Many states, including Wisconsin, have laws prohibiting leaving firearms within easy access of a child.

Chapter Four

is away from the storage location, the firearm is of no benefit.

Quick-access safes are recommended for nighttime storage of firearms. Although the handgun is rapidly accessible to users with the required code, children do not have easy access to the weapon.

Final Considerations

No system is perfect—each has advantages and disadvantages that must be considered by the user. People who have been carrying firearms for a long time usually have a box full of discarded holsters. Depending on body type, behavior, dress code, size/weight of the gun, and many other factors, users will eventually discover a method that works best for their situation.

Drawing from a Holster

Once the user has selected a method to carry the handgun, a significant amount of practice must be invested learning how to safely draw the handgun. The proper draw must be practiced until safe methods are used without conscious thought. Shooting oneself in the leg as a result of an improper draw will not assist in the defense against an attacker!

Furthermore, people who carry a handgun for defense are encouraged to carry the handgun in a consistent manner. Although it may not be practicable to always carry the handgun in the exact same location, this should be a routine that is violated only with hesitation. If a person carries a handgun using five different methods, it's unlikely that person has sufficiently practiced all five draws to the point of "unconscious

Chapter Five

competence."[16] Furthermore, it's very likely they may forget where they're carrying their handgun when faced with a sudden surprise attack.

Regardless of the type of holster being used, the universal rules of firearm safety must be obeyed when drawing a firearm. Specifically, the gun must not be pointed at anything the user is not prepared to destroy, and the trigger finger must remain outside the trigger guard until the user wants to discharge the weapon.

Keeping the weapon pointed in a safe direction is a key component of the draw. This is relatively easy when using a typical belt holster, but becomes more complex with specialty holsters and downright difficult with shoulder holsters. No matter what holster type is used, the gun must not point at any part of the user's body during the draw.

The other universal rule consists of keeping the trigger finger outside the trigger guard until the user intends to fire the gun. Some users place their finger on the trigger before they want to fire, in an effort to gain speed. In fact, beginning to pull a revolver's trigger during the draw used to be taught in police academies. It was called "prepping the trigger," with the theory being that the shot would be fired just as the gun reached full shooting stance. However, there are real safety issues with this technique.

First of all, it presumes the handgun user will shoot someone. Adoption of this technique would require two separate draws—one with the finger on the trigger, and one without—necessitating a decision-making process. This could lead to a delayed and/or slower draw, as the defender attempts to

---

[16] "Unconscious competence" is the final stage in the Four Stages of Competence, described in the Glossary.

Drawing the Handgun

decide (or never decides) which draw to use. Finally, the situation may have changed since the time the defender decided to draw. If the attacker moved, or is no longer visible, or for some other reason shooting is no longer justified, the defender has been planning to shoot from the moment the draw decision was made. How likely is it the decision can be countermanded? Based on recent reaction-time studies, it's not very likely.

Second, under a "fight-or-flight" stress response, dexterity and coordination will be decreased. Even if the defender intends to shoot from the moment the draw begins, prepping the trigger makes it more likely the defender will fire a shot into the ground—or into their own leg during the draw—than if they had used normal trigger finger discipline. Instead of saving time, as originally intended, the "trigger prep" has the potential to unsafely discharge ammunition. Besides the obvious hazard, this is ammunition that might be needed later in the gunfight.

No matter what the type or location of the holster, the user must keep the handgun pointed in a safe direction during the draw, and not place their trigger finger into the trigger guard until it is intended that the weapon fires.

When initially practicing the draw, the user must begin with an unloaded weapon. Until the user has gained the necessary practice and experience to become intimately acquainted with the draw, the potential for an unintended discharge is far too high to risk using a loaded weapon. In addition, users should start slowly and concentrate on performing the technique slowly and correctly. The mantra, "Slow is smooth, smooth is fast" is very applicable here. Performing the skill slowly and correctly will lay the neural pathways later used to perform the correct skill more quickly.

Chapter Five

If the gun is dropped while practicing, *do not attempt to catch it*. Allow the gun to land on the ground. Most quality handguns are "drop-safe," meaning they will not fire when they hit the ground. The few quality guns that could fire if dropped require a fall from several feet off the ground onto a hard surface, with either the muzzle pointed down (causing the bullet to be fired straight down) or a blow to the hammer. These are relatively unlikely. An attempt to catch a firearm, on the other hand, runs the risk of inadvertently inserting a finger or thumb into the trigger guard. The trigger is then pressed during the "clutch" phase of the catch, sending a bullet out the barrel.[17]

Drawing and Movement

The user should only draw their handgun when faced with the potential of death or great bodily harm. Given those circumstances, the first step of drawing the firearm is this: Move to cover! When faced with a situation in which the defender might be injured or killed, the preferred response is not being there anymore. Thus, upon recognizing the need for the gun to be in the hands, the defender should begin moving away from the threat and/or towards something that will prevent the assailant from completing the attack.

While training, movement is incorporated into the draw by side-stepping anytime the handgun is brought out of the holster. At close range, a side-step may be enough to get off the line of attack temporarily; at long

---

[17] A Montclair, California police detective was accidentally shot while trying to catch a dropped pistol, and a San Fernando officer, found dead, may also have suffered the same fate.

Drawing the Handgun

range, the side-step is the first step towards cover or concealment. Movement will be discussed further in the chapter on Tactics.

Drawing from a Holster

The basic concepts of a safe draw are best learned by starting with the standard belt holster. The concepts practiced there can then be transferred to other holster types with appropriate practice.

Belt Holsters

Begin the draw by stepping towards cover or to create distance from the attacker. Always take a side step at a minimum, to ingrain movement as part of the presentation of the weapon.

While taking the side step, the defender clears any concealment garment away from the handgun so the strong hand can properly grip the gun. Whether the strong or reaction hand clears away the garment depends on the clothing worn by the defender. If the concealment garments worn can always be reliably cleared away with the strong hand, this method is preferred. The strong hand clears the

Strong hand grasps gun while reaction hand moves to chest.

clothing away from the handgun grip by hooking it away with the thumb or cupping it away with the fingers. This leaves the reaction hand free to engage in other tasks, such as deflecting blows, pushing a family member out of the way, etc. If the reaction hand isn't needed for any of these

Chapter Five

activities, it is brought to the user's chest. This placement ensures it will not be swept by the gun muzzle during the draw.

If the defender wears any concealing garments that cannot be consistently and reliably cleared with just the firing hand, the reaction hand should be used to clear away the concealing garment. A reliable draw is as important as a reliable handgun—a "malfunction" of the draw is potentially deadly if the defender's weapon cannot be brought to bear when needed.

Use of the reaction hand to clear away a concealing garment.

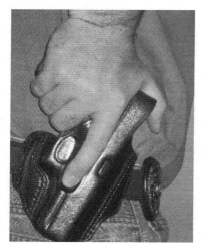

Full firing grasp obtained while the gun is still in the holster.

When the clothing has been cleared away from the handgun, the strong hand immediately takes a full "firing" grasp on the weapon. Note: the trigger finger remains outside the trigger guard, but the rest of the grip is established just as if the gun was being held for firing. This prevents having to re-adjust the grip after the gun is removed from the holster. Trying to change the grip after the gun is drawn slows down the draw and could

Drawing the Handgun

result in the gun being dropped.

To orient the hand on the gun, recall the position of either the middle finger under the trigger guard, or the web of the hand under the gun's tang. Either of these landmarks can be used to ensure the gun is grasped the same each time it is drawn.

If the holster has a thumb snap or safety strap, it is released after a grip landmark has been grasped. *Holsters that require a release that cannot be achieved from a firing grasp are not recommended for defensive use.*

With the gun in a firing grasp, it is drawn directly upwards out of the holster. When the gun clears the holster, the muzzle is rocked forward so it is aiming downrange towards the intended target. Meanwhile, the drawing arm is brought as high as possible, until the gun is near the armpit. When the gun is high, it is thrust straight and level towards the target. "Bowling" or "swooping" the gun towards the target from below adds time and causes vertical misses because the user, subject to an adrenaline dump, commonly forces the gun past its target. Vertical movement has no built-in stop, while a "thrust-out" draw naturally stops at the appropriate point.

Gun up and pointed forward; reaction hand sliding to gun.

The reaction hand is slid across the body and brought to the handgun as the gun is brought forward. At no time does

Chapter Five

the muzzle point at or "sweep" the reaction hand. Incorrect performance of the "smack," when the hands are brought together, can lead to self-inflicted gunshot wounds.

In order to develop maximum speed, start slowly and eliminate any extraneous movement. The hips and shoulders should not move during a stationary draw (though they may move while the user is moving to cover). Any such extraneous movement merely slows the draw.

The trigger finger remains off the trigger until the user intends to discharge the weapon.

Reholstering the handgun is performed exactly in reverse. The trigger finger is placed outside the trigger guard as soon as firing ceases. The gun is brought back towards the strong side shoulder, with the reaction hand sliding onto the chest as the gun is brought back. The gun is then lowered to the holster, still pointed downrange, until the top opening of the holster is contacted by the bottom of the slide or barrel. This contact can be used to guide and rotate the handgun to line up with the holster. Before the gun is inserted, re-check that the finger is off the trigger and place the strong-hand thumb on the back of the hammer or slide. The thumb can detect any cocking of a double-action hammer, and ensures the slide remains fully shut on striker-fired guns in tight holsters.

Holstering should be performed with one hand and without looking at the holster. The user's vision should remain on the potential threat while the gun is being reholstered. Having to look at the holster is a sign that the process has not yet been fully mastered.

Be certain the finger is outside the trigger guard, and do not wear clothing that could catch or snag the trigger as the gun is inserted into the

Drawing the Handgun

holster. For example, clothing with drawstrings or toggle fasteners near the waist could be forced against the trigger while holstering. If the finger or any other object remains inside the trigger guard, the trigger may be pressed to the rear and the gun can discharge.

Shoulder and Cross-draw Holsters

Shoulder holsters share most of the basic concepts of the belt holster. Begin to move to cover as the draw begins.

While the strong hand is grasping the handgun in the holster, the reaction arm must be brought up to avoid sweeping the arm during the draw stroke. The best way to do this is to perform a high block, as if someone were trying to strike the defender's head. After the gun has cleared the reaction arm, the reaction hand is then brought to the two-handed grip. Care must be taken to avoid placing the reaction hand in front of the muzzle.

Photos 1-3: drawing without sweeping the defender's reaction arm.
Photo 4: re-holster, stabilizing the holster while not sweeping the reaction hand.

Chapter Five

Reholstering almost always requires two hands with a shoulder holster. The gun is placed into the holster as far as possible with the reaction arm again held high to avoid sweeping the muzzle across the defender's body. However, to fully seat the handgun in the shoulder holster, the reaction hand is usually required to stabilize the holster while the strong hand finishes inserting the gun. So, after the muzzle has entered the holster as far as possible before holster shift becomes a problem, the reaction hand stabilizes the holster, and then the handgun is fully inserted. The muzzle must not sweep the user's hand or body at any time during the reholstering process. As always, the user must be certain the trigger finger is outside the trigger guard and that no object can possibly enter the trigger guard while reholstering, to prevent an accidental discharge. Reholstering requires practice so the user can be certain the muzzle isn't sweeping their own body, while still keeping their own vision on the potential threat.

Ankle Holsters

As mentioned, ankle holsters have one significant disadvantage—they immobilize the user during the draw. It is impossible to be moving to cover or away from an attacker while drawing from an ankle holster.

There are two methods of performing a reliable draw from an ankle holster—either dropping to one knee, or performing a very large side-step and reaching down to the ankle. The preferred method should be based on the user's flexibility and what they find to work best with their combination of gun, holster, and clothing.

To perform the kneeling draw, the user drops to the strong side knee while the reaction hand pulls up on the reaction side pants. The strong hand

Drawing the Handgun

grasps the handgun butt and performs the draw. As the handgun is raised towards the threat, the reaction hand joins the strong hand in a two-handed grip. If the opportunity presents itself, the user should get to both feet *without looking down or using a hand to balance.* If this is impossible, the user should definitely avoid ankle holsters.

To perform the side-step draw, the user's reaction hand grasps the reaction side pant leg while the user takes a very large side step to the reaction side. This side step should be more than twice shoulder width. The user then bends at the waist and reaches across the body to the reaction side ankle to draw the weapon with the strong hand.

Side-step draw.

This method has the advantage of staying on both feet for mobility once the draw has been completed, but it requires increased flexibility and makes it somewhat more difficult to watch the threat.

Reholstering is best accomplished by kneeling. This provides better stability for an unhurried job. Be certain no object—including the trigger finger—is inside the trigger guard when the handgun is reholstered. Again, sufficient practice is required so the gun can be safely holstered while the user's attention is on the potential threat.

Chapter Five

Pocket Holsters

Pocket holsters are somewhat similar to belt holsters. The primary difference is the user must be sure the pocket holster remains in the pocket when the gun is drawn. Furthermore, depending on the size of the gun and the size of the pocket, it may not be possible to obtain a full firing grasp on the handgun while it is in the pocket. A fist takes up more room in a pocket than a semi-curled hand. The user might not be able to fully form a fist around the handgun grip and still withdraw the gun from the pocket. Additionally, guns with hammers are more likely to snag when being drawn from the pocket.

To prevent this, the thumb is not wrapped around the grip in the pocket, but is instead left on the back of the handgun's hammer or slide. This prevents the hammer or slide from catching on the edge of the pocket, and leaves the hand narrow enough to more easily be removed from the pocket. As soon as the thumb clears the pocket, it is then wrapped around the grip and the draw proceeds just as a belt holster would.

Some pocket holsters have an edge that is designed to catch on the corner of a pocket, to keep the holster within the pocket. Users should practice with their particular holster to determine whether the draw must "hug" one side of the pocket in order to "catch" the holster. This tends to be required more with tightly fitted leather holsters (which do a better job of breaking up the gun's outline) than sticky but loose fabric holsters (which release the gun but don't conceal the outline as well).

Reholstering to a pocket holster is usually best done by taking the holster out of the pocket, carefully placing the gun into the holster, and then inserting the combination into the pocket. It may be possible to safely

Drawing the Handgun

reholster the handgun directly, again depending on the combination of gun, holster, and clothing.

It is important that nothing else ever be kept in the pocket besides the gun and holster. If another object is in the pocket, it could activate the trigger while the gun is being inserted or reholstered.

Abdominal Packs and Tucked-In Holsters

Fanny packs and tucked-in holsters require a two-handed draw. The reaction hand opens the compartment or removes the concealing garment while the strong hand grasps the handgun. The user must be certain the handgun doesn't sweep the reaction hand during the draw.

Reholstering with any of these holster types is not a speedy process and will almost always require two hands. The reaction hand reveals and opens the holster, while the strong hand inserts the handgun. These holsters require extra care to avoid sweeping the reaction hand or body.

Purses and Day-Planners

Drawing a handgun from a purse or day-planner is a three-step process. The reaction hand begins by stabilizing the purse. The strong hand begins by opening the compartment (by sliding the zipper, releasing the Velcro, or unsnapping the fastener). Then the strong hand reaches in, obtains a firing grip on the weapon, and releases the thumb break (if present). Finally, the weapon is withdrawn.

Reholstering is not a speedy process and requires two hands. The reaction hand stabilizes the purse while the strong hand inserts the handgun. Extra care is required to avoid sweeping the reaction hand or body.

Chapter Five

Tactics

The ability to shoot a handgun accurately is an important defensive element. However, use of proper tactics during a deadly encounter is even more crucial. Stopping the assault is good. Not getting killed is better. But stopping the assault *while* not getting killed is best!

Situational Awareness

Before a person can defend themselves against a threat, the threat must be recognized. Therefore, the most important tactic is to be aware of the environment and people surrounding one's self. Environmental awareness is the most important skill for avoiding dangerous situations. The best way to deal with a potentially lethal encounter is to be somewhere else when it happens! Carrying a pistol gives a person the means to defend themselves

Chapter Six

against a violent assault, but putting one's self in a position where such an assault is a predictable occurrence is a potentially deadly mistake. The best rule of thumb is this: if you wouldn't go there if you *weren't* carrying a gun, don't go there when you *are* carrying a gun.

Jeff Cooper popularized a color-code system[18] which describes the appropriate mental state of a defender in different environments. In condition "White," the defender is oblivious to their surroundings or any potential danger. If the defender were attacked while in White, they are at such a disadvantage they will likely be annihilated. In condition "Yellow" the defender is aware of their environment and on the look-out for potential danger, although there is no identification of any specific threat. In Yellow the defender is aware that a threat may exist and is observing their environment to locate any such threat. In condition "Orange" the defender has identified a specific potential threat, and is presumed to be taking action in response to that threat—avoidance, distraction, verbalization, drawing a handgun or pepper spray, or whatever their risk assessment deems appropriate. Finally, in condition "Red" the defender has realized the specific, immediate danger of death or great bodily harm and is only concerned with winning the ongoing lethal encounter.

If a person is not in a completely secure environment they should be in Yellow. Yellow is neither paranoia nor fear of everyone around you. Instead, it acknowledges the world is not an inherently safe place. Yellow is a calm, even placid outlook, while remaining aware of surroundings and environment. An individual in Yellow recognizes potential hazards and

---

[18] Jeff Cooper's Commentaries, Vol. 4 #2 and Vol. 13 #1.

Tactics

avoids them, while someone in White is likely to stumble right into the middle of an unrecognized problem.

Confronting a Threat

When the defender recognizes a threat and transitions to condition Orange, it may be appropriate to draw the handgun without shooting immediately. There may be times when the handgun is drawn in preparation or with advance notice. In cases where it isn't necessary to fire immediately, the handgun should be brought to a "low ready" position.

Handgun at low ready

Grip the handgun as if shooting, but position the handgun close to the body instead of using extended arms. The trigger finger remains outside the trigger guard until a decision has been made to shoot, and the handgun is kept pointed in a safe direction—low is best—to safely stop any bullet that is accidentally fired.

This placement brings the weapon into a prepared position that maximizes the safety of bystanders while preparing the handgun for immediate use should it be needed. It gives the defender full view of the assailant's hands, which are the most dangerous part of the assailant's body. It is the hands that kill, not the eyes, so the focus must be on the hands. Furthermore, the low ready position keeps the handgun close to the defender's body for better weapon retention options.

Chapter Six

If it is necessary to shoot immediately upon drawing, the low ready position is bypassed and the gun brought directly towards the target.

Verbalization

While drawing the pistol the defender should shout, "Drop the weapon!" loudly and aggressively. This "verbal stun" may accomplish several things. It may surprise the assailant as well as informing them their potential victim is not just going to submit quietly; it tells the attacker how to prevent being shot; and its volume and message will attract the attention of anyone in the area, creating witnesses that can testify about what they observed.

Verbalization must be practiced along with the draw so it becomes a programmed response. Used automatically, without thought, it doesn't delay the actions of the defender. "Drop the weapon" is used because it will work in most defensive situations and can be "programmed," whereas a message customized for the situation requires processing and analysis. Shooters who customize messages almost always wait until the end of a sentence before firing. Finishing a sentence delays the defender's response and is undesirable, whereas playing an automatic programmed loop doesn't cause a delay.

Defenders should strive to practice clear, specific commands. "Alpha" commands, such as, "Drop the weapon!" give the assailant clear directives and exhibit confidence on the part of the defender. "Beta" commands, such as, "Don't make me shoot you!" show weakness and indecision, and do not provide specific directives.[19]

Forcefully shouting, "Drop the weapon!" while drawing a handgun and moving towards cover may dissuade an assailant. Had the assailant expected such a response, it's likely he would have selected a different victim. Unfortunately, not all assailants will be discouraged.

Target and Target Areas

Before shooting, the defender must be certain the *perceived* threat is an *actual* threat. As described in the fourth rule of firearms safety, "Be sure of your target and what's beyond." There are far too many examples of defenders mistakenly shooting innocents or family members. A bullet, once launched, cannot be recalled.

Consideration should be given to where to aim the shots. In a defensive encounter, the sole purpose of shooting is to stop the attack as quickly as possible. An assailant will stop their attack when they are unable or unwilling to continue. The assailant will cease their attack for one of three reasons: psychological factors, unconsciousness, or immobility.

Psychological factors are unpredictable and cannot be counted upon. If the assailant tries to press home their attack even after the defender produces a weapon, verbally stuns the attacker, and begins moving assertively towards cover, he's not acting rationally. An irrational attacker may very well continue the attack even after shots are fired, and even after receiving injury from bullets. That leaves only two ways to ensure an assailant stops

---

[19] Force Science Research Center, Force Science News #43.

Chapter Six

attacking: rendering them unconscious or immobile. This directly bears on the desired target area.

Central Nervous System

The quickest way to end an assault is to shut off the attacker's central nervous system—the system that controls the attacker's body. This can be accomplished by shooting the assailant in the brain or upper spinal cord. This is the preferred method because it causes an instant cessation of the attack. However, the brain is relatively well-protected by thick bone in some parts of the head. To maximize the likelihood of the pistol bullet penetrating sufficiently, the bullet should be centered in a two-inch band between the eyebrows and the tip of the nose. Hits higher than the eyebrows might be deflected by the skull; hits lower may pass under the brain (although if they impact the spinal cord they will still be effective).

Center Mass

The central nervous system can be a relatively difficult target to hit, especially when the target is moving or the range is farther than five yards. In those cases, the defender should concentrate on placing bullets into the attacker's upper chest. This is a larger target that will cause unconsciousness after the assailant has lost enough blood. Be aware, though, that unconsciousness as a result of blood loss can take a *long* time. In a famous FBI shootout in Miami in 1986, a bank robber received a fatal wound to his aorta early in the gunfight. He fought on for more than two minutes, even though he was losing blood the entire time, before he was stopped with shots to the head. Causing blood loss is effective but potentially time-consuming; thus the preference for central nervous system shots.

Tactics

Pelvis

Some instructors suggest shooting the assailant in the pelvis instead of the head because the pelvis is a key component of mobility. Breaking pelvic bones may immobilize the attacker, giving the defender a tremendous advantage. Even if bones are not broken, there are major arteries in the pelvis that, if hit, will cause significant blood loss. Finally, the pelvis is a more stable target than the head, less subject to bobbing around in a fight.

These arguments are valid but must be weighed against other factors. Handgun rounds—particularly small-caliber cartridges—are not particularly good at fracturing thick bone. Major pelvic bones are heavy structures and bullets may simply make a hole, or ricochet off, instead of breaking them. Immobilizing the attacker is good, but having the attack stop instantaneously is even better. As a target area the pelvis has some advantages, but it is not an area without drawbacks.

No matter which target area is preferred, there will be situations where that area is not exposed. In those cases, shoot the attacker in whatever body part they make available. If the head is available shoot it. If the head is too difficult a target for any reason, shoot the attacker's upper chest or pelvis. If the upper chest is concealed or not available as a target, shoot at the center of whatever body part the assailant presents.

Cover and Concealment

In a deadly assault, the defender should make it as difficult as possible for the assailant to attack. One of the best ways to do this is to use any available cover or concealment. "Cover" is any object that will stop a bullet; for example, a telephone pole, thick tree, or landscaping wall.

Chapter Six

"Concealment" is anything that conceals the defender, even if it may not stop bullets; for example, a hedge, darkness, or the wall of a house.

The use of cover should be programmed into the defender to the point they feel uncomfortable if they're exposed to the target. In police training officers are trained to shoot around cover; by beginning their handgun instruction shooting around barricades, officers are programmed to feel uneasy when not behind cover.

Training in use of cover cannot be overemphasized. A tragic example of a lack of programming in movement-to-cover is available by watching the in-car video of the 1992 murder of Georgia State Trooper Mark Coates. Trooper Coates was an excellent, fit officer wearing a bullet-resistant vest. When attacked by a gun-wielding suspect, Trooper Coates repeatedly shot his assailant, striking the suspect with five of six rounds—exceptional accuracy in such an incident. Unfortunately, Trooper Coates did not immediately seek cover, instead standing exposed to the subject who then fired a round between Trooper Coates' vest panels. After being struck by the bullet Trooper Coates moved to cover, but it was too late—his wound was fatal.

Only by thorough programming of the use of cover will the defender remember to seek it during a lethal encounter.

Using Cover

Do not crowd the object being used as cover. Instead, leave a *minimum* of a foot between the muzzle and the object being used as cover. More distance is generally preferred. As an example, if using the corner of a brick wall, step back from the corner five feet or so. This permits full arm extension while keeping the muzzle a foot away from cover. Increasing the

Tactics

distance between the defender and cover is even better, because the defender has more reaction time should something unexpected appear around the corner. Although it's instinct to feel better protected when close to the object providing protection, the increased reaction time is very valuable.

When shooting around cover, expose only as much of the body as necessary to shoot accurately. This should be only the eye, the handgun, and as much of the arm and head as necessary to aim and fire the shot. Do not expose half the body, but only the bare minimum required for defense.

In order to maximize the effectiveness of cover, it's usually better to shoot around cover, not over it. This exposes less of the head to incoming bullets. To illustrate this point, observe someone using a mailbox as cover. Have the defender use their index finger to aim and "shoot" over the mailbox. How much of the defender can be seen? Then have the defender point their finger from around the mailbox, exposing only enough to aim and "fire" their finger. Less of the defender is exposed, as shown by the pictures below.

Shooting around cover reduces the exposure of the defender.

Chapter Six

"Slicing the pie" is a shorthand term describing how best to utilize cover when looking around a corner or searching for the location of an assailant. To slice the pie, rotate around the axis of the "pie" until the target comes into view. To make maximum use of cover, the defender stops moving around the angle when the target becomes visible. A diagram of the defender's area of vision created by the defender's movement resembles pie slices when viewed from above.

Defender's viewpoint as defender moves to the left, adding "slices" of view to what can already be observed. As the defender moves, more area comes into view until, at last, the "target" table comes into view.

Using Concealment

Concealment ranks second only to cover as an effective defense mechanism. It's more difficult to attack a person that cannot be seen, so a defender's survivability is increased if concealment is utilized.

Experience shows that some attackers would not shoot through a piece of paper held in front of the gun muzzle.[20] Clearly a simple piece of paper won't stop a bullet, but the visible barrier adds psychological inhibition to the attack. Although this isn't the sort of statistic a person would want to bet their life on, defenders should use any advantage or psychological barrier available to them, including this phenomenon, to impede the attack.

The interior walls of most homes serve as concealment, as they are relatively ineffective at stopping bullets. Bushes are another example of objects that may conceal the defender, making attack more difficult, but that wouldn't stop a bullet. The defender should use any available concealment to their advantage, as it makes the defender harder to attack.

Traversing Left and Right

When beginning to use cover and concealment, it becomes quickly apparent that it's difficult or impossible to utilize the textbook shooting distance and make maximal use of cover. When multiple assailants, unexpected angles, and sudden attacks are considered, it's clear the defender will be forced to shoot in other directions than simply forward off an established base.

---

[20] Street Survival: Tactics for Armed Encounters, p. 183.

Chapter Six

The ability to traverse, or turn the upper body side-to-side, is one of the reasons for the development of the stance described in Chapter Two. By isolating the upper torso and aiming platform from the hips and legs, traversing is as simple as rotating the upper body. The shooting platform is unchanged. Thus, a defender can simply rotate their upper body to address a threat to one side or another, instead of having to take the time to move their feet into another position. Besides reducing the chance of tripping over an unseen obstacle, it reduces the time between targets, giving the defender the ability to fire more quickly.

The amount of traverse available to the defender depends on their physique and coordination, but is generally about 180 degrees (90 degrees left and 90 degrees right). By bending one or the other arm at the end of the traverse, it's possible to increase the angle further. If the gun is rotated onto its side, still more rotation is possible.

Clearly at such extreme angles it's desirable to eventually reposition the feet. No one is at their best when trying to fight 110 degrees from the direction their feet are pointed. But the speedy response to threats from an unexpected direction is valuable.

Foot Movement to Change Direction

Having recognized a threat from an unexpected direction, the defender will generally desire to face it directly. To do so, step forward with the foot away from the threat, pivoting on the foot closest to the threat. For example, to turn 90 degrees to the left, the left foot pivots in place while the right foot steps forward and around to bring the body into the desired alignment.

The "away" foot is brought forward instead of the "near" foot stepping back. This movement is more assertive and less likely to cause a fall on an unseen obstacle. Humans have much better balance moving forward than rearward, and stepping forward combines psychological and physiological advantages.

The independence between the upper and lower bodies becomes even more useful as the defender begins assertive movement over distance, in order to reach cover or increase the distance between themselves and the assailant.

Movement

Movement is a survival factor as important as cover and concealment. Movement takes the defender to cover; makes an attack more difficult or even impossible to carry out; interferes with the attacker's plan; and provides situational advantages to the defender.

For example, assume a defender is walking from a garage to the entrance to their home. Seeing a knife-wielding attacker come around the corner of the house, the defender should immediately move towards a position that interferes with the attacker's ability to carry through the attack. This might be around another corner or behind a bench, to place barriers between the attacker and defender. Or, perhaps the defender can reach a doorway in time to prevent the attacker from entering the building. If nothing else, a moving target is more difficult to attack than a stationary target. In any case, the defender should immediately begin moving off the line of attack.

Chapter Six

Movement has already been incorporated in the system described in this book. The defender's side-step during the draw accomplishes two things. It begins the defender's movement towards the protection of cover, and it moves the defender off the "line of attack."

The line of attack is the path through which the attack is carried out. A simple exercise illustrates the concept. While holding an imaginary knife, have a role-player rush a defender from about 30 feet away. As the attacker accelerates they commit themselves to a specific path. Changing direction becomes increasingly difficult as the attacker gains speed. If the defender takes a large correctly-timed side-step, the attacker will find it difficult to reach the defender and carry out the "attack" as they rush by. A simple side-step has been reported as helpful against an attacker who is suffering tunnel vision. A large side-step may take the defender out of the attacker's field of view, leaving the attacker wondering where the defender went. Even if the side-step doesn't have the dramatic effect of these two examples, it still takes the defender out of the space the assailant is attacking, forcing the assailant to change their aim or direction and forcing the attacker to react to the defender's action.

Movement and Cover

After the defender has drawn their gun and begun their movement, how should further movement be incorporated into the defender's actions? The purpose of movement will vary depending on the exact situation and environment of the defender, but the defender should be moving any time they are not behind effective cover.

Tactics

If the defender is behind effective cover, they should generally remain there using the cover to fullest advantage.[21] If the defender isn't behind cover the defender should be moving towards it for several reasons.

First of all, movement towards cover will eventually obtain cover for the defender. Second, a moving target is more difficult to hit than a stationary one, so even if the defender isn't behind cover, they are less likely to be shot than if they are standing still. Finally, movement forces the assailant to change or modify their action, interfering with the attacker's OODA Loop.[22] All of these things are good as they make the assailant's attack more difficult.

Although it is generally desirable to increase the distance between an attacker and defender, there can be situations in which the opposite is true. For example, in situations where innocent people are in or near the line of fire, the defender might advance directly towards the attacker. Attacking the attack is a generally unexpected response that may disrupt the attacker's OODA Loop. Although it makes the defender an easier target, the attacker also appears larger in the defender's sights. In combination with the OODA disruption, this can be surprisingly effective.

Moving and Shooting

Whether the defender should shoot while moving depends on several factors. Based on the circumstances of the event, does it make more sense to simply sprint to the destination, thereby reducing the time exposed to the

---

[21] One exception would involve multiple assailants attempting to outflank the defender.

[22] OODA = Observe/Orient/Decide/Act, as described by Col. John Boyd, USAF.

Chapter Six

threat? Or would the defender be better served by putting the attackers under fire and possibly disrupting their attack?

The first time a defender practices moving while aiming a gun, they will immediately notice one difficulty: the handgun seems to point everywhere except at the target. The bouncing induced by the defender's movement can challenge the defender's ability to put rounds into the assailant—and accuracy is everything. "You can't miss fast enough to win." Without hits, a handgun is nothing except an expensive noisemaker.

Techniques have been developed that minimize the gun's motion during the defender's movement. While it is impossible to eliminate all of the gun's motion, these techniques take out the worst of the bouncing and allow better accuracy. Each of these techniques incorporates isolation between legs and torso as developed in the shooting stance. The two most useful techniques are the "Groucho" and the "S.A.S." techniques.

The Groucho is named after Groucho Marx, as it resembles his rolling stride. It's based on using the legs as shock absorbers to soak up the worst of the bumps, and rolling the feet from heel-to-toe to minimize the disturbance caused by the feet impacting with the ground. To perform the Groucho, flex both knees so they are moderately bent. Step forward and roll onto the heel of the foot, continuing to roll the foot forward until the foot rolls forward off the toe. Continue this with each foot, moving forward as smoothly as possible and using the knees to isolate shocks. Though effective, this technique is tiring over long periods.

The S.A.S. method differs significantly from the Groucho. Instead of walking in an unusual gait, the S.A.S. has the defender walking normally. However, when the defender wishes to shoot, the defender begins taking very small "baby steps" at the same pace they were formerly walking. After the shooting is completed, the defender resumes their normal gait. The advantage to the S.A.S. is it is not tiring to move an extended distance and the amount of gun movement while firing is decreased. This may provide increased hits on the assailant, which is good. However, its disadvantage is that it nearly immobilizes the defender while they are shooting, making them an easier target to attack—particularly risky at close range. Furthermore, most self-defense scenarios will not involve lengthy hikes where the defender must be prepared to instantaneously shoot.

Both the Groucho and S.A.S. methods have advantages and disadvantages. Because different physiques and physical abilities play into the effectiveness of each technique, the defender should experiment with both methods and decide which is generally right for them.

Traversing While Moving

While moving in one direction, it is possible to rotate the torso left or right to engage a target in another direction off the line of movement. The technique is the same as stationary traversing, with the exception of gun movement introduced by movement over ground. Thus, the defender can move to cover in a direction other than directly ahead, while simultaneously engaging the assailant with gunfire.

When shooting while moving, the defender must remain careful to fire accurately. Though this is more difficult while moving, a defender cannot afford to miss. Hits must be obtained or the gunfire is not only ineffective, but dangerous to the public and general citizenry. Fire only as fast as accuracy allows.

Chapter Six

Is the Threat Over?

After drawing a handgun, verbally stunning the attacker, moving aggressively towards cover, and possibly shooting the assailant, the defender must stay mentally focused on the fight until the threat is known to be over. This might be because the attacker is down and unable to continue the assault, or because the attacker has fled. There are several critical steps to follow before lowering one's guard and assuming the threat has ended. Relaxing too soon is foolhardy.

Scan 360 Degrees

Even after the initial threat appears unwilling or unable to continue the attack, the defender must assume there are accomplices nearby. If the defender has not yet reached cover, finish getting there while checking for other assailants. There are multiple assailants in about 50 percent of police-involved shootings.[23] Multiple assailants should be anticipated, even if only a single attacker was first identified and neutralized. It's relatively common, for example, for armed robbers to plant accomplices in their target area. If a defender engaged an armed robber in a bank or convenience store, the defender should be prepared for attack by the "seeded" accomplice(s). If more assailants are present the defender must continue their defense.

To check for other assailants that may still present danger, lower the gun to a low-ready position, ensure the trigger finger is outside the trigger guard, and bring the handgun back towards the body. This provides for improved weapon retention and decreased ability for an unseen attacker to seize the

---

[23] Street Survival: Tactics for Armed Encounters, p. 204, and other sources.

weapon. Consciously eliminate tunnel vision (quite likely to be present after an adrenaline dump) by scanning for the initial assailant, and then 360 degrees for other threats. Sweep the eyes left and right past the known attacker. Then the defender performs a full 360 degree scan by turning left and right as far as possible, looking over their own shoulders, to ensure everything around them has been scanned. The defender should consciously examine the surroundings to determine whether anyone is carrying a weapon, approaching, or shooting.

It may seem like such a scan is excessive—how could the defender be unaware that another assailant is shooting them? However, under extreme stress it is common for the body's inherent defensive mechanisms to activate. Some of the side effects of these defense mechanisms include tunnel vision, auditory exclusion (decreased or absent sense of hearing), and reduced pain sensitivity (so the defender may be unaware of injuries they have received).[24] Unless the defender practices performing this scan, it is likely it will not occur during a critical event.

Multiple Assailants

As mentioned, multiple assailants are common. This has obvious advantages for the attackers. However, because this situation is predictable, tactics that mitigate this advantage can be practiced and used by a defender.

First of all, it is again imperative that the defender be aware of their environment and act assertively as soon as the threat of assault is recognized. Allowing one's self to be boxed-in by multiple assailants puts the defender

---

[24] Deadly Force Encounters, p. 49.

Chapter Six

far behind the curve and makes it more difficult to regain the initiative. In condition Yellow, the defender must be aware of attempts to box-in, cull-out, contain, or isolate the defender. Upon recognizing any of these tactics, the defender must act immediately and assertively to prevent their completion. As always, the best plan of action is to prevent the situation from reaching a point where the assailants believe a physical assault may be successful.

If the defender is in a position where they are facing multiple assailants, the odds are stacked against them. The best tactic is to turn the fight into a series of "one-on-one" encounters, instead of allowing it to continue as a many-against-one fight. Movement is a key factor. If it is available, the defender should move to cover where the attackers cannot outflank the position. If such cover isn't available, the defender should move relative to the attackers in an attempt to put them in line with each other. Thus, ideally the defender only has to counter one attack at a time. This makes it difficult or impossible for all the assailants to attack simultaneously, and increases the efficiency of the defender's response.

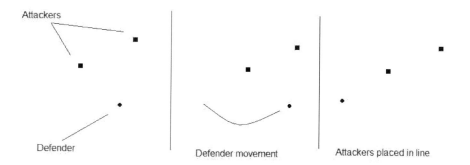

In some situations it may not be possible to put attackers in line, or the defender may already be behind effective cover. When presented with multiple assailants, the defender should shoot the attacker that puts the defender at most risk. This will vary by situation. A knife-wielding attacker six feet away is more dangerous than a shotgun-armed opponent 30 feet away, while a rifle-armed assailant 50 feet away is probably more dangerous than a pistol-armed attacker 20 feet away. An attacker approaching within arms-length is almost always most dangerous because of their ability to physically attack and try to interfere with the defender's ability to defend against *any* of the attackers.

Close-Quarter Distances

Using a handgun against an assailant who is within arm's reach requires different techniques. Utilizing the "standard" two-hand would place the defender's handgun within easy reach of the attacker, with the likely result of a wrestling match over the gun. Since struggling over the gun makes it more difficult to shoot the assailant, and because the assailant could potentially win the struggle, it is highly desirable to avoid this.

At close quarters, the defender must keep the handgun tucked close to their body instead of extending it in front as normally done. This tucked-in position has several disadvantages: it makes it impossible to use the handgun's sights; it is less accurate; and it's much easier for the defender to accidentally shoot himself. However, the advantage of making it more difficult for the attacker to take the weapon away makes these disadvantages acceptable.

While the defender draws the handgun, the defender's reaction-side arm should be placed at about head height and kept close to the defender's own body. This allows the defender to block or divert attacks against their own head, and ensures their own arm will not be struck by their own bullets.

Chapter Six

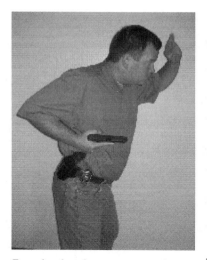

Reaction hand up; gun rotated away from body.

The defender, as always, should also take an aggressive step to the side to get off the line of attack, and then keep moving in an effort to keep the assailant off balance. The direction of this movement is situation-dependent, but it should rarely be backwards, away from the assailant. The assailant can move forward more quickly than the defender can move backwards, and a person moving forwards has the advantages of better balance and the ability to see where they are going.

After an initial side-step, the defender may be able to finish moving to the attacker's side or rear, making the attack more difficult. If the defender cannot achieve that, movement straight into the assailant may be the best option, if it has the possibility of forcing the attacker backwards or off balance.

While keeping their reaction hand high, the strong hand draws the handgun up out of the holster and immediately rotates the muzzle towards the assailant. The top of the handgun should be rotated away from the body to prevent the slide or hammer from catching on the defender's clothing. The handgun should be aimed into the assailant's chest—which may be quite an upward angle, depending on the proximity of the attacker. Alternatively, the defender may choose to target the attacker's pelvis in the hopes of removing the attacker's ability to stand. As mentioned earlier, pelvic shots are not a sure thing and have some disadvantages. In any case, the defender should not target the attacker's abdomen. The abdomen is void of most critical target areas, and shots here are least likely to stop the attack.

Determining the proper angle to fire shots requires practice. Many shooters find it difficult to shoot high enough at a close-range target to ensure hits to the chest. Some defenders face limitations on dexterity and/or agility, making such an aim point impossible. Therefore, the defender must practice this shooting enough to reflexively know how high to hold; or if chest shots are not practical, how low to hold to hit their chosen aiming point.

The defender should then begin firing while still moving. Use the reaction hand to block attacks to the head while simultaneously moving towards a position of advantage.

The danger of a close-in attack is intense, and readers may recognize that the suggested model leaves the defender's chest and abdomen somewhat open to assault. However, when an attacker has been allowed to close in, few options remain—particularly against an attacker who may be stronger than the defender. By protecting the head, the defender is most likely to remain conscious and able to mount a defense, and least likely to shoot their own arm or hand (such as might happen if the defender attempted to push away the attacker).

One alternative that is frequently taught is the "Speed Rock," wherein the defender aggressively pushes back the attacker with the reaction hand, while simultaneously taking a large step backwards and drawing the pistol. Some also propose the defender lean backwards to assist in firing high into the chest of the attacker. In theory, this creates distance from the attacker,

Chapter Six

gives the defender the time to draw their own gun, and places rounds high in the attacker's chest.

This works well on the shooting range, but has limitations that prevent its recommendation on the street. First of all, it presumes a defender large enough to propel an attacker backwards while only using their reaction hand. It also presumes a flat surface where the defender's large back step can be taken without loss of balance or running into a solid object. It presumes the attacker doesn't start forward immediately, taking advantage of the defender's off-balance posture. Finally, if the defender does not immediately withdraw their reaction hand, the defender may shoot himself if rounds are properly aimed into the attacker's chest. (This risk can be somewhat lessened by a variation wherein the defender palm-strikes the attacker's chin, but the other disadvantages remain.)

As such, stepping off the line of attack and protecting the head is recommended as a more universal technique over the "Speed Rock."

Shooting with One Hand

There will be times when both hands are not available. One example of such was the close-quarter assailant, discussed above. There can be other times when both hands are not available, such as when the defender is opening a door, pulling their child away from danger, or a hand is injured because of the assault.

It is important for the defender to be able to operate and fire their handgun with either hand, singly. Although two-handed firing is greatly preferred for speed and accuracy, force-on-force drills have consistently shown that the hands are frequently struck by an opponent's bullets. In a

Tactics

shooting situation, it's very possible a defender's hand will be struck by the assailant's gunfire.

To effectively shoot with one hand, keep the same stance as before. Do not turn sideways to the target, as some target shooters do. While this posture may seem to offer a thinner target to the assailant, it allows an assailant's bullets to pass through multiple critical areas of the chest. For example, if a person is shot front-to-back, it's impossible for a single bullet to strike the heart, aorta, and both lungs. Indeed, a bullet would have to be extraordinarily well-placed to strike more than one critical area, front-to-back. However, if the defender is shot from the side, one bullet could indeed strike all four critical areas, causing more serious injury.

One-hand stance, gun rotated towards centerline for increased strength.

The defender should hold the gun just as the strong hand does in a two-handed hold. The non-firing arm can be brought to the chest, for stability, or if injured, stabilized in the belt or clothing. The handgun is brought up normally, though many people prefer to rotate the entire firing arm inwards (counter-clockwise when held in the right hand; clockwise when held in the left hand). This inward rotation slightly stiffens muscles in the forearm and may make recoil recovery somewhat more positive. This technique works for either the strong or reaction hand.

95

Chapter Six

Drawing with the Reaction Hand

Drawing the handgun using only the reaction hand can be problematic if the holster is worn in a non-ideal location or the defender's physique prevents adequate reach. To practice, the defender must use an unloaded gun. As stated before, if the gun is dropped, do *not* attempt to catch it in midair.

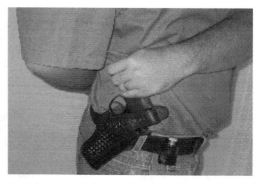

Gun being withdrawn far enough to allow 180 degree rotation so firing grip can be achieved.

The first step is to expose the holster and release any retention strap in place. Then, grasp the handgun in a firing grip. If it is not possible to grasp in a firing grip, rotate the gun in the holster 180-degrees so a firing grip can be obtained. Then draw the handgun from the holster, being careful to avoid sweeping the muzzle across any part of the defender's body.

Positioning the holster where it can be reached by either hand is preferred. For example, a belt holster placed at three o'clock on the body can be reached across the front of the body more easily than one positioned at four o'clock. However, it might be possible to reach behind-the-back for a holster at four o'clock. These holster placements

After firing grip is achieved, gun is drawn from holster.

Tactics

must be individually determined based on physique, flexibility, and concealability.

A reaction-hand draw can be nearly impossible with some holster types. For example, a gun carried in a pocket holster is very awkward to draw with the opposite hand. If the defender is carrying a backup gun, this may be the preferred weapon. Ideally, the backup gun would be easily accessible to the reaction hand as well as the strong hand, in case the strong hand is disabled.

One-Hand Emergency Reload

The defender must not only be able to draw and fire with one hand, but be able to reload their handgun with one hand as well.

To perform a one-hand emergency reload of a semi-automatic pistol, holster the gun with the slide still locked back. If a belt holster isn't being worn, the weapon can be held between the legs. Retrieve the full magazine and smartly insert it into the magazine well, being careful not to knock the gun out from where it's being held. Grasp

Inserting a loaded magazine into holstered handgun—slide still locked back.

the gun in a firing grip and release the slide. If the pistol's slide release is inaccessible or the slide is closed, the slide can be racked by sharply running the rear sight over the heel of a shoe, the belt, or any other solid protrusion that is available.

Chapter Six

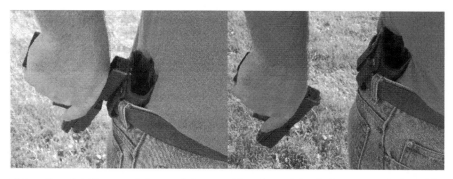

Using the pistol's rear sights and the outside edge of the holster to rack the slide. Note the slide is racked fully to the rear, with the handgun continuing forward past the holster to ensure the slide is not "ridden" forward.

To perform a one-hand reload of a revolver, a somewhat similar method is used. The firing hand releases the cylinder latch, which is pressed open with the firing hand or by pressing the side of the cylinder against the leg. The revolver is inverted and the ejector rod is activated. Ideally the ejector rod is pressed against the underneath of the injured arm; if that's not possible, either the firing hand must shift its hold to reach the ejector, or a nearby surface can be used. Finally, the revolver is tucked into the waist with the cylinder open, and the firing hand inserts cartridges into the cylinder. The cylinder is pressed closed, and then the revolver is drawn from the waistband (being certain the trigger finger is outside the trigger guard).

One-Hand Malfunction Clearance

Malfunctions are somewhat more likely when a semi-automatic pistol is fired with one hand, because the handgun is not braced as well as when it is fired with two hands. Semi-automatic pistols require a solid hold so the recoil energy is directed into the operating mechanism. If held loosely or fired with an unlocked wrist, some recoil energy is absorbed by the

Tactics

defender's wrist and/or arm, and insufficient energy remains to properly work the action. This is more prevalent when the gun is fired with only one hand.

The best course of action is sufficient practice in one-handed shooting, including practice from non-traditional and awkward positions, to ensure the pistol still functions correctly. However, if the pistol malfunctions, it must be returned to working order as soon as possible.

Perform the Phase One clearance by forcefully seating the magazine. While ensuring the trigger finger is outside the trigger guard, forcefully pound the butt of the gun into the thigh to seat the magazine. Then rack the slide by dragging the rear sight against a solid protrusion, such as a belt or heel. The ejection port should be clear of clothing or other blockage while doing this, so any faulty round can be cleanly ejected without being pushed back into the ejection port.

Seating the magazine during a one-hand "Phase One" malfunction clear.

If the Phase One process doesn't fix the malfunction, the defender must perform a Phase Two malfunction clear. Kneel. Eject the magazine by thumbing the release button while striking the wrist on the bent knee. If this is done sharply enough, the magazine should be flung from the gun. Rack the slide at least three times by dragging the rear sight against a solid protrusion, such as a heel or holster edge. Grasp the gun between the legs or place it in the holster, and insert a new magazine, ensuring it is fully seated. (Because the slide is closed, the magazine will be more difficult to seat.)

Chapter Six

After the magazine is seated, rack the slide using the rear sight again, and the gun should be back in service.

Low Light Environments

Studies of defensive shootings show the majority of them occur in low light surroundings. Seventy percent of police shootings occur in hours of darkness.[25] Upon reflection, this makes sense—criminals prefer the dark where their activities are less likely to be seen and detected.

Low light situations can be encountered even during daylight hours. Entering a dimly-lit basement or warehouse, or investigating a noise in a closet, takes the defender into areas where their vision is impeded by lighting conditions.

Low light environments present their own set of challenges to a defender. It can be more difficult to detect people. When a person is observed, the defender must determine whether the person is an actual threat or an innocent bystander. At home, perhaps the noise was caused by a family member moving about the home or returning home late at night. Even if the suspect is identified as hostile, the defender must still determine whether the attacker presents a danger of death or great bodily harm. This can be particularly difficult in low light, as it's more difficult to see the attacker, what they're holding, and what they're doing.

Although low light situations are more challenging, the defender remains fully responsible for identifying the target. Sadly, there have been

---

[25] SureFire Instructor Handbook, p. 20; and Law Enforcement Officers Killed and Assaulted, 2005, USDOJ, Federal Bureau of Investigation.

several cases where a family member shot an intruder, only to find out the "intruder" was a son or daughter coming home late at night.[26] These shootings are the result of failing to identify the target and its threat before engaging in gunfire. The suspect *must* be positively identified as an assailant posing imminent threat of death or great bodily harm before a shooting is justified.

Low light tactics cannot be adequately addressed in only a few pages— the topic deserves an entire book itself. However, an overview of applicable techniques, to acquaint the reader with the theories involved, would include the following generalizations.

If the darkness can be eliminated by turning on lights, it's often wise to do so.

Using a Flashlight with a Handgun

Flashlights allow a defender to identify a suspect, but also pinpoint the defender's location. If forced to search their surroundings, the defender should "strobe" the flashlight, turning it on and off quickly and repeatedly. In addition, vary its angle and direction as much as possible. Although there may be little doubt as to the defender's approximate location, such flashlight use is disorienting and helps conceal the *exact* location of the defender. With practice, this technique is surprisingly confusing and disorienting.

---

[26] A Connecticut police officer shot his 18-year-old daughter as she snuck back into the house, reported May 30, 2007.

Chapter Six

When searching, be aware of the ambient lighting conditions. The defender should avoid being backlit, as it reveals the defender's exact location and makes for an easy target.

When the defender locates a suspect, the defender should "power with light" to take away the suspect's vision and determine whether the suspect has a weapon. If shooting is justified, the defender should shoot using the light, then shut off the light and move to another position. This should be repeated as needed, while keeping the light's "on" time to a minimum to reduce the time the attacker has to locate and target the defender. The technique is "light-on, shoot, light-off, move" rapidly enough so any return fire directed at the flashlight's location misses the defender. If shooting is not required, use the light to disorient the suspect and escape.

The flashlight selected should be a quality flashlight designed for tactical use. The $5 plastic light found at a local hardware store is not suitable for this task! The flashlight must be bright enough[27] to blind a suspect; sturdy enough to survive drops; waterproof so it functions after being exposed to water; and have a suitable momentary switch so it can be "strobed" effectively. With the introduction of LED lighting, the flashlight market is changing very rapidly. This makes a listing of suitable flashlight models and brands out-of-date almost as soon as it is printed, but examples of appropriate lights would definitely include most of the Surefire™ line (including the relatively inexpensive G2), some of the Streamlight™ line, the Gladius™ by Blackhawk, etc.

---

[27] 60 lumens is a good baseline for indoor use.

With training and practice, it is possible to use a handgun and flashlight simultaneously and effectively. The flashlight may either be held in the reaction hand, or may be mounted to the handgun.

When held in the reaction hand, the flashlight may be aligned with the handgun using several possible techniques. These include the Harries, Sure-Fire/Rogers, Ayoob, FBI, and Neck Index techniques. Each technique has strengths and weaknesses.

Weapon-mounted lights are an option for users who desire a dedicated light. While these lights allow the defender to shoot more effectively, most limit the strobing effectiveness when conducting searches. The buyer is advised to try both, preferably under an instructor's tutelage, and determine their own needs and preferences.

Fighting In and Around Vehicles

With the amount of time spent in and around motor vehicles, it's important for a defender to understand a few basic realities about vehicles. Simply put, vehicles are both a method of escape route and a trap, and the defender must understand the capabilities and limitations of vehicles to maximize the vehicle's usefulness and minimize the inherent dangers.

As always, the defender's first line of defense is awareness of their surroundings. When approaching a parked vehicle, is anyone lounging about for no perceptible reason? Are the vehicle keys already in the hands to minimize the amount of time spent standing motionless between vehicles? Was the vehicle parked in a well-lit area that provides good observation of the surroundings? Does the driver scan the interior of the vehicle before entering?

Chapter Six

Once inside the vehicle, does the driver immediately lock the doors to prevent someone from easily entering the vehicle? Does the vehicle quickly drive away to minimize the amount of time spent trapped in a motionless vehicle?

While driving, are the vehicle's doors always kept locked so no one can easily enter the vehicle when the it is parked or stopped at an intersection? Are windows kept rolled up far enough to prevent someone from forcing an arm inside? When stopped in traffic, does the driver leave at least a car-length in front of their vehicle as an escape route to drive ahead, left, or right? Or does the insufficient space in front of the vehicle allow a following vehicle to block the vehicle's movement and trap the vehicle where it sits? Is the driver prepared to aggressively use this escape route when a person approaches with a weapon? Or will the driver delay until the suspect is outside the driver's window, effectively trapping the defender motionless in the driver's seat?

If appropriate, a car is a much more effective deadly weapon than a mere handgun. If an individual standing in front of the car presents a deadly threat, drive over them. If the deadly threat is at a distance to the side, the vehicle is an excellent escape mechanism. Even with a flat tire, the vehicle can take the defender from the scene much more quickly and safely than any alternative method. However, the vehicle becomes more of a trap if the assailant is standing next to the driver's window—hence the importance of situational awareness, to avoid this.

Shooting In and Around Vehicles

Vehicles can serve as moderately effective cover against handguns. If escape is possible, the driver should lean over as far as possible, using the doors for concealment, and aggressively drive away.

If necessary, can the defender draw their weapon while seated? Some holster types make this more difficult. For example, front pants pocket holsters are difficult to access, while shoulder holsters and ankle holsters are easier. Belt holsters vary based on physique and placement, while cross-draw holsters come into their own.

Do not engage in a rolling shoot-out as seen on TV. Though this makes for exciting action films, shooting from a moving motor vehicle is incredibly irresponsible. Not only is it unlikely to be effective against an attacker or their vehicle, but bullets fly everywhere—and the defender is responsible for every one of them. Shooting from a moving vehicle should generally be left for the movies.

Handgun rounds will penetrate all the glass on the auto, although windshield glass is tough enough to somewhat deflect handgun rounds. Vehicle bodies are inconsistent performers against handgun rounds—though they will usually at least slow down the projectiles. The more auto body panels between the defender and attacker, the better.

If the vehicle is immobilized, the defender should immediately exit to prevent being trapped inside. If possible, exit the side opposite the direction from which the attack is coming. Utilize the car as cover between the assailant and the defender. As with all cover, shoot around or under the car, not over it. The best parts of the car for cover are the engine block, the axle, transmission, and tire rims.

Chapter Six

Mindset

So far this book has addressed two of the three pillars of the combat triad. Physical skills and tactics are two of the three key components necessary to win an armed confrontation. However, alone they are not enough. The third pillar—mental preparation—is absolutely required to win the encounter.

A civilized society encourages its members to engage in non-extremism. People are encouraged to share; to see the other person's point of view; to negotiate; to settle differences peacefully; to talk and act in moderation; and in other ways to "play well with others." This is the preferred method of interaction in a polite society. This fails miserably as a defensive mindset, however, because the typical criminal assailant is *not* a rational member of a polite, civilized society.

Chapter Seven

Examine the "typical" violent attacker. According to U.S. Department of Justice statistics, 82 percent of violent crimes are committed by males, and 44 percent of violent crimes are committed by people younger than 25 years old.[28] Examining criminals that have murdered police officers, 95 percent had previous criminal arrests.[29] Thus, a "typical" attacker is a fairly young male with an extensive criminal history. The threat of future prosecution is probably not much of a deterrent. He sees victims as "prey" and himself as a "predator." This seems natural to him.

These assailants have been described as "animals." This dehumanizing term is unpleasant to polite, civilized individuals. And while such a term may be frowned upon, it succinctly describes many of the motivations and outlooks of violent attackers.

What civilized person forcibly rapes women? What rational person threatens innocent victims with death for the $20 in their pocket? To some degree, the humanity of these assailants is legitimately questioned. Certainly they think and act differently than people who accept the social construct of a civilized society. Though they move through that society, they are not part of it.

When viewed impersonally, from a distance, we can coolly and objectively examine the criminal and his violence. We can detachedly understand what may have formed such a criminal, and even feel pity for the person placed in that situation. We can feel sorry for the innocent babe subjected to a dysfunctional family, abuse and/or sexual assault, drug

---

[28] Crime in the United States, 2005, tables 33, 41.

[29] Law Enforcement Officers Killed and Assaulted 2005, *Officers Feloniously Killed* overview.

dependency, gang violence, and a slew of other factors that influenced their choices in life. Such empathy is the product and luxury of a civilized person.

Massad Ayoob likens criminals to wolves.[30] He uses the apt analogy that criminals in today's society are like wolves a hundred years ago. It may be pleasant to contemplate them from a distance, or while they are safely caged in a zoo. It's much different when a hungry wolf is stalking you as prey.

During an attack civilized empathy is worse than useless, because empathy slows you down. In the moments between recognition of imminent violence and the resulting injury or death, the defender does not have the luxury of detached contemplation. The victim acts, or is violently overcome. Gunfights are time-competitive and distractions are a very serious handicap.

There is no soft, kind defense against a slashing blade or a skull-crushing hammer. The defender must perform brutally, in order to prevent brutality to themselves or their loved ones. The defender must act immediately and aggressively, as stopping a violent attack requires countervailing violence. Street fights are not fair. Death awaits a defender who isn't aggressive enough in defending the life of themselves or a loved one. The defender must fight without reserve, without thought of pain or injury, without reluctance to do serious harm to their attacker. To survive, the defender must act decisively and without hesitation.

Training and practice must emphasize this mental preparation and mindset, because for many people it is the most difficult thing to achieve. Unless they have witnessed the aftermath of a violent attack, or experienced

---

[30] The Truth About Self Protection, p. 4

Chapter Seven

it themselves, it can be difficult to comprehend the savagery and speed of the event. If the defender must learn this during the event, and then find and adopt the appropriate mindset, the defender will be overcome.

I witnessed an example of this in a police class. An officer was briefed on the training scenario—stopping the rampage of a man with a gun. I knew the officer had excellent pistol skills and knew proper tactics, and the officer entered the situation knowing exactly what he would find. And that officer, who should have won the scripted encounter, was "killed" within five seconds of the start of the Simunitions FX™ exercise. He was lackadaisical, apparently expecting even more warm-up time than had already been provided. And he didn't enter the gunfight with the mindset necessary— that he was going to *fight without hesitation or quarter*.

The danger of unexpected attacks is incredibly high, explaining the importance of situational awareness as discussed in Chapter Six.

Mindset Exercises

Exercising the mind is as important as exercising the body. A mind that hasn't practiced guiding and directing its own activity will be as unsuccessful as an unpracticed arm trying to throw a ball. Learning to throw takes repetition. Laying neural pathways allowing the brain to function better under stress is the same. Why would something difficult—like keeping mentally focused while someone is trying to kill you—be easy to perform without proper practice?

Mindset

Positive Self-Talk

First of all, the defender must believe they can win the encounter. Police officers are trained to use positive self-talk to ingrain the proper mindset found most effective in lethal encounters. In a relaxed state, prior to beginning duty, officers will repeat a personalized version of this mantra example:[31]

- I will survive every encounter
- I know the necessary tactics
- I am talented with my handgun
- I can stay focused on what I must accomplish
- I can perform deep breathing exercises to control stress
- I can choose not to feel fear
- I can defeat those who attack me
- I can shoot to save my life or the life of my loved ones
- I can keep fighting, no matter what, even if I am injured

Note that every line is simple, to the point, and positive. Negative wording, such as, "I won't give up", is not used as it suggests giving up is a possibility. "Try" is never used because it also implies failure is possible.

Daily repetitive exposure to these self-directed statements can program them into the subconscious. Because a person's behavior is shaped by their own expectations and self-perception, this positive self-talk can have significant benefit.

Breathing Exercises

Breathing properly seems too simple to require explanation. After all, if breathing were being done improperly, the person would pass out or hyperventilate, right? In actuality, though, trained breathing exercises can

---

[31] Adapted from The Tactical Edge: Surviving High-Risk Patrol, p. 36.

Chapter Seven

enhance the defender's mental state and ensure their body is functioning with a proper oxygen supply.

Defenders who haven't practiced breathing exercises often begin hyperventilating under stressful situations. Hyperventilation results in physiological changes which reinforce the stress the body is experiencing. This results in a self-defeating loop that diminishes the defender's ability to remain focused on the task. Watch someone going through a haunted house. Although they're under no physical exertion, their psychological stress results in rapid breathing, and that hyperventilation reinforces their anxiety. How well could a defender in that psychological and physical state defend himself? The same thing—except more intense—happens to police officers hunting a gun-wielding criminal. Though the police might have merely walked through two rooms, they sound as though they've just run a marathon.

Mental focus is retained through proper self-control, which can only be obtained with proper control of breathing. The defender must consciously practice proper breathing techniques to program breath control and psychological stabilization.

Perhaps the simplest technique available is to inhale through the nose and exhale using a "hissing" sound.[32] This requires a full intake of breath instead of shallow panting. It also ensures the air remains in the lungs long enough for oxygen exchange to take place.

---

[32] Ken Good, Strategos Int'l.

Mindset

Another technique, useful after a stressful incident, is the four-count relaxation technique. Breathe in for four counts; hold the breath for four counts, and exhale for four counts.

Both of these techniques must be practiced until they're second nature in a fight. For example, upon recognizing danger the defender should begin moving aggressively to obtain a position of maximum tactical advantage. While doing so, the defender breathes in deeply through the nose to fuel their body for fighting or fleeing. Inhaling deeply through the nose and exhaling through the teeth will ensure maximum oxygen utilization prior to heavy exertion, while possibly adding to the disorientation of the attackers. After all, who expects their prey to begin hissing?

If the four-count relaxation exercise is practiced on a routine basis it will work to reduce the stress level experienced post-defense. Having programmed the relaxation response before it's needed through physical rehearsal and practice, the relaxation technique will be available to the defender when needed after crisis.

Mental Rehearsal

Positive self-talk and the ability to mentally focus are key components of proper mindset. These components are even more helpful to a defender who already has practical gunfighting experience. A study of World War II pilots showed that pilots who survived their first few air-to-air engagements were likely to survive the duration of their tour.[33] Because most people will never be in an actual gunfight, gaining personal experience is somewhat difficult.

---

[33] SureFire Instructor Handbook, p. 46.

Chapter Seven

(Range exercises and target shooting are important physical skills, but are *not* gunfighting.)

The ability to successfully withstand a lethal attack can be greatly increased by mental rehearsal. Mental rehearsal is a method for visualizing performance before physically performing the task. Thus, the person has "practiced" their response to a lethal threat without having actually suffered such an attack. The defender is better able to execute a proper response and thus more likely to be successful than a defender who was unpracticed.

It might seem unlikely that mere mental visualization can have profound benefits. <u>If the defender doesn't have the physical skills to perform what has been visualized, such skepticism is deserved</u>. If the mental rehearsal bears little resemblance to reality, skepticism is well-deserved. However, with the physical skills in place to carry out what has been appropriately mentally rehearsed, the defender gains tremendous benefit. After all, mental rehearsal is a tool frequently used by Olympic athletes, world-class shooters, sports stars, and public speakers.

Mental imagery is a powerful tool that allows the defender to rehearse their response to a lethal threat. Mental rehearsal isn't mere daydreaming. Instead, it is a focused teaching session in which the user practices their behavior in a specified environment. Mental rehearsal is not a substitute for physical practice, but it enhances and reinforces the ongoing training.

To perform mental rehearsal, a quiet place is found where the practitioner can enter a relaxed, receptive state of mind. Deep breathing exercises assist in attaining this receptive state. The user then imagines a situation they may encounter—a person appearing around a corner with a knife, an assailant kicking in the front door of the house—and concentrates on feeling the sense they are actually experiencing the event. Then, the user selects an effective response that they are capable of performing. The user sees herself making the precise physical moves required to perform the task, following through the process until the situation is successfully resolved.

Like a cardiovascular workout, mental rehearsal must be repetitive to be effective. Three sessions a week, of about 20 minutes each, are ideal, though less is still beneficial. Furthermore, it's imperative that the practitioner actually knows the correct tactics and responses and has the physical skills to implement what has been visualized. Again, it's not a case of "practice makes perfect." Instead, *"perfect* practice makes perfect." Visualizing the incorrect method of performing a task simply reinforces bad behavior.

It's important to mentally rehearse a variety of situations, and different responses on the part of the attacker. Although an assailant might break off an attack upon recognizing an unexpected defense, others may not. Ralph H., a DEA agent in Mississippi, describes what not to expect when confronting a criminal at gunpoint:[34]

"Normal people are upset and compliant when a gun is pointed at them.

A criminal, especially one who is far enough into it to be doing something to you that would cause you to pull a gun out, is not a normal person.

We are taught to arrest dangerous subjects with our guns drawn. This is not to scare or intimidate them, but merely to gain an advantage if it is necessary to use deadly force.

---

[34] Quoted with permission, March 2006.

Chapter Seven

The biggest mistake a citizen can make is to try and figure out how a criminal scumbag is going to react, based on how he, a normal person, would react, to any situation. They are truly in a different world from the average taxpayer, and they usually have a lot less to lose than you do. They do not have the respect for life, property, or the rights of others, that you do. They do not have the moral compass that you have, and they will not behave as you would behave.

This is one of the things that training from any reputable gun school is going to teach you and IMHO, is much more valuable than any marksmanship or tactics training you will receive at the same time.

You are betting your life against theirs. The only difference is you are betting a million dollars, and they are betting 25 cents."

Mental rehearsal is a technique that can allow a defender to have experienced—to some extent—a gunfight instead of it having to be a new experience. This is a significant benefit to the defender.

Training Adjuncts

Mental rehearsal is useful to mentally prepare for a gunfight. Simulation training—when properly administered—can provide gunfight experience without the real-world consequences—like risk of injury or death. Notice that simulation training *must be done correctly to avoid harmful, incorrect training that is detrimental to defensive skills. Perfect* practice makes perfect. It's better to not train via simulations than to train incorrectly with them.

Simulation training puts the student in a realistic situation or setting that could be predictably encountered in real life. Then, using non-lethal training aids, the defender handles the scenario to the best of their ability. Following the simulation, the defender and instructor debrief to review the defender's performance and the lessons that can be learned.

The simulation training usually includes a pain penalty to reinforce the lesson if the defender is shot. For example, the defender will wear required safety equipment over the eyes, face, throat, and groin, but only a t-shirt and light pants. The sting of the "wound" helps to ensure that these training activities are taken seriously.

Some of the tools that can be used for simulation training include Simunitions FX™ and AirSoft™ projectile weapons, inert pepper spray, and Shocknife[35] or chalked training knives. These tools allow a person to simulate a lethal encounter and learn the applicable lessons without risk of permanent injury. FX rounds are usually available only to government or military purchasers, although some training companies offer them. Other manufacturers are reported to be developing similar technology that may be more widespread. AirSoft guns are inexpensive and widely available. They can be adapted to replicate the function of the defender's chosen handgun.

Simulation training has incredible benefits, but it has significant downfalls as well. This training is incredibly valuable because it can be used to teach important lessons and test the student's ability to implement previous lessons under stress. Because it is so effective at ingraining the material being taught, the lesson objective must be tactically sound and the trainer's role-players carefully scripted to ensure the correct lesson is administered.

---

[35] http://www.shocknife.com

Chapter Seven

If simulation training is conducted poorly or without proper planning, the session can be harmful as it reinforces bad behavior and poor tactics. Even worse than incorrect instruction is the risk of serious injury or death if safety procedures are lax. Students have been killed in "simulation" training when proper protocols were not used or enforced. It is absolutely vital that simulation training is conducted by a qualified instructor who understands the educational and safety protocols required to perform sound training in a safe environment.

Post-Shooting Actions

When the defender believes the attack is over, they should move to cover and immediately perform a full 360-degree scan as described in Chapter Six. If a complete scan does not identify any further potential threat, the defender must act to secure their post-shooting survival—both personal and in the courtroom.

Immediate Tactics

If no further threats are immediately recognized, the defender should de-cock their pistol (if it's double-action), finish moving to cover, and reload the weapon in preparation for additional threats. Perhaps the assailant's partner will come around the corner a minute from now, wondering what is taking the attacker so long. Perhaps the getaway driver will investigate to

Chapter Eight

see what happened. Or maybe the assailant's family member, who had been watching from a distance, will enter the scene bent on revenge. In any case, it's beneficial to have a fully-loaded weapon to defend against possible further attacks.

Tactical Reload

It is extraordinarily rare for a defender to be able to count the number of rounds fired in a gunfight. This is understandable given the number of things to concentrate on when thinking itself may be difficult. It is quite common for defenders to believe they have only fired one to three rounds when they actually fired six or more. Thus, training should include the idea that ammunition should be replenished during a lull in the encounter, rather than at the inopportune time when the gun actually goes empty. This replenishment during a lull—the tactical reload—maximizes the number of rounds available to the defender in case action resumes. The tactical reload differs from the emergency reload as the gun is not empty when the tactical reload is performed. Therefore, after shots have been fired—even if the defender believes only a few were discharged—the gun should be reloaded if a lull in the action occurs, or the encounter seems to be over. This might be after the attacker falls down and ceases the attack, or after the attacker has fled. It is not during the actual attack.

There are two main schools of thought regarding the tactical reload. One school teaches that every round of ammunition should be conserved, because neither the number of adversaries nor the number of rounds still required can be predicted. This school encourages exchanging pistol magazines at the gun's magazine well—a task requiring practice and dexterity to perform. The other school believes exchanging magazines near

Post-Shooting Actions

the gun while experiencing an adrenaline dump requires more dexterity than may be available. Instead, this school recommends removing and stowing the first magazine, then reloading with the new magazine. This is a simple technique and only differs from the emergency reload in that the original magazine is retained instead of being dropped. Based on the principle that simple is generally best, and that fewer universal techniques are generally preferable to multiple specialized techniques, the second method of tactical reload is recommended.

Pistol Tactical Reload

After moving to cover and scanning for further threats, release the pistol's magazine and pull it from the magazine well. Place the partially-expended magazine in a pocket. Retrieve the spare magazine in the same way an emergency reload is performed, and *firmly* seat the magazine. Be certain it is in place, because with the slide closed additional force is usually required to fully seat the magazine. Failure to fully seat the magazine may cause the magazine to misfeed or unexpectedly fall out of the gun.

When practicing this technique, the defender should always place the partially-full magazine in the same pocket. In that way, the defender will know where to retrieve the magazine should its ammunition be needed. If the defender only carries one spare magazine, the original partially-depleted magazine may be transferred to the magazine carrier after the pistol is reloaded.

Revolver Tactical Reload

Revolvers are much less conducive to tactical reloads. It takes a fair amount of dexterity to reload a partially-full cylinder. After an adrenaline

Chapter Eight

dump, this will be even more difficult. It is easier to simply eject everything and replace it with a full load. To perform this, kneel down after moving to cover and scanning for further threats. Perform an emergency reload. After completing the reload and closing the cylinder, glance at the cartridges on the ground. If any are live cartridges, pick them up and place them in a pocket.

After completing the pistol or revolver tactical reload, again scan the environment for threats.

Scene Actions

After the defender has moved to cover, performed a tactical reload, and confirmed no more threats are detected, the defender should reholster their handgun and summon the police. The defender must remain ready to draw the handgun again if the assailant shows signs of renewing their attack. It is undesirable to have the police arrive and find the defender with a gun in their hand—not because the defender has something to hide, but because it makes it more likely the defender might be shot by responding officers. This risk can be mitigated by holstering the handgun and by communicating with responding officers before and during their arrival.

Do not approach the assailant(s) to render first aid. Although the attacker may have stopped shooting or may even appear unconscious, the defender has no guarantee the attack will not resume. Perhaps the attacker is lying in wait to ambush the defender when approached to render aid. Police are taught that a minimum of two officers are required to safely approach and secure a potentially lethal threat—and officers are equipped with bulletproof vests and handcuffs. Let the police secure the assailant.

Post-Shooting Actions

Summoning aid for the attacker is extremely important, however. It shows the defender had no desire to kill the attacker, and only wanted to stop the threat on the defender's life. Failing to summon aid, on the other hand, shows a mindset of utter disregard for human life. The best way to summon aid for the attacker is to call the police and report the incident.

Immediately ensure police are dispatched to the scene. Under no circumstances should the defender avoid involving the police. If no phone is available and no bystanders are known to be present, shout, "I'm going to call the police," and then immediately go to a phone and do so.

Dealing with the Police

It's very beneficial for the defender to get their message to the police as soon as possible. If the defender is the one to contact police, they should say something similar to, "There has been a shooting at [location]. Send an ambulance and the police. The suspect is wearing [clothing]. I was attacked by the criminal. I'm wearing [clothing description]."

If a family member or friend accompanies the defender, that person should greet the officers outside the area of the attacker/defender. This gives the greeter an opportunity to brief the officers and describe the defender.

When the police contact the defender, they are likely to have guns drawn and pointed. The defender must immediately comply with all directives and orders from the police. Do not argue or hesitate, but simply do what the police officers say. *Under no circumstances should the defender hesitate to drop their handgun. Under no circumstances should the defender turn towards the officers with a gun in their hand.*

Chapter Eight

The defender should tell the police they were attacked by the assailant, and point out the assailant's weapon, any accomplices, and any witnesses. The defender need not admit they shot the assailant, but it's definitely in the self-interest of the defender to give the police information that shows why the defender acted as they did. Then the defender should say something similar to, "I want to cooperate with your investigation and I'll make a full statement after I've met with my attorney." The defender should then exercise their right to silence. As traumatic an experience as this may be, avoid running off at the mouth at the scene.

Some people debate whether the defender should make an immediate statement to the police or retain an attorney before making a statement. It is almost certain the defender will be arrested if no immediate statement is provided—the police cannot *assume* a justification for the defender's use of lethal force. However, there is a strong argument for retaining legal services prior to making statements that could be used against the defender in court. Criminals have a right to speak to an attorney before speaking to the police. In such a serious situation the defender may want to take advantage of that same right, even if the phone call to the attorney must be made from an interview room or a holding cell.

Physical Reactions

After the effects of the adrenalin dump begin to wear off, it's common for the defender to experience several startling side-effects. These might include nausea, diarrhea, hyperventilation, dizziness, heightened emotional response, or any number of other physical or psychological responses.[36] No

---

[36] Deadly Force Encounters, p. 180.

individual's reaction can be predicted with certainty. Some people suffer several symptoms while others have mild or unnoticed side-effects. Having these experiences is common, however. These reactions are a significant reason why a defender might elect to consult with an attorney before making a statement. The delay gives the defender time to regroup and recover from some of these physical reactions.

Other Factors

The defender's handgun will be seized as evidence until the investigation is complete. Depending on the nature and seriousness of the attack, the defender's clothing may also be seized, along with a blood sample. If the police don't request such a blood sample, the defender should consider requesting one be taken to show they were not under the influence of alcohol or drugs at the time of the incident.

It's possible the assailant will file a civil lawsuit against the defender. The defender may sue the assailant as well, of course, but often the assailant has no assets worth seizing. Consult with a lawyer and your insurance carrier regarding civil lawsuits.

Shooting an assailant is almost guaranteed to be an expensive and grueling proposition. The defender's actions will be investigated as a crime to determine whether the defender was warranted in using lethal force. And the defender's actions will be second-guessed by people who didn't see the attacker in action. Contrast that with the long-term psychological and physical injuries—or death—resulting from an attack that *wasn't* thwarted. Although each individual must decide their own course of action, I know the

Chapter Eight

value I place on my life and the lives of my loved ones. If necessary, I *will* use deadly force to save them.

Selecting a Defensive Handgun

Equipment is frequently over-emphasized in defensive training. Having said that, good equipment makes the defender more efficient and capable, while poor equipment can hinder performance.

When considering what handgun to purchase there are many factors to consider. The prime factors include reliability, controllability, size, weight, and effectiveness. Other factors may include rust resistance, ease of maintenance, safety features, and cost.

Examination of the prime factors reveals why they are most important. Reliability is king for any defensive handgun. A handgun *must* work when it is needed. Although no mechanical device is perfect, the defender's life depends on their selected handgun's reliability. Any handgun that isn't 100 percent reliable must be fixed, or replaced with one that is dependable.

Chapter Nine

Controllability is another key factor. The defender must be able to control the handgun in order to shoot well. As an extreme example, small .44 Magnum revolvers may be powerful and reliable, but are so difficult to shoot quickly and accurately that they are seldom the best choice.

Size and weight are factors that must be considered as well. An example might be the large steel high-capacity .45 handguns that many people enjoy shooting. These handguns may be controllable and effective, but their size and weight demand specific clothing styles for reasonable concealment.

Finally, effectiveness must be considered. Effectiveness is usually judged on the basis of caliber. Different handguns fire different sizes of ammunition; generally, a handgun that fires a larger or faster bullet is more effective than a handgun firing a smaller or slower bullet.

Types of Handguns and Actions

There are two basic kinds of defensive handguns—revolvers and semi-automatic pistols.[37] Revolvers contain their ammunition in a revolving cylinder. Pistols contain their ammunition in a removable magazine located in the grip.

Revolvers and pistols share common trigger mechanisms. These mechanisms can be roughly divided into three similar types: "single-action," "double-action," and "double-action-only."

---

[37] Although "pistol" is sometimes generically used to refer to any handgun, it technically refers to handguns that contain the fired cartridge within the barrel. In this book, "pistol" refers to semi-automatic handguns (all of which fire the cartridge in the barrel); "handgun" is used when differentiation between revolvers and pistols is not needed.

Selecting a Defensive Handgun

"Single-action" guns require the hammer to be cocked before each round can be fired. On a revolver, the shooter's thumb performs this action, while on a pistol a reciprocating slide does it.

"Double-action" refers to guns where the hammer may be cocked in two ways: either manually with the thumb, or by pressing the gun's trigger to fire the gun. When the trigger is used to cock and fire the

Smith & Wesson double-action-only revolver.

gun, the weight of the trigger pull is higher than on most single-action guns. This may help prevent inadvertent firing but makes accurate shooting somewhat more difficult. Double-action revolvers use the trigger to cock the hammer for each shot. Double-action pistols only require the first shot to be trigger-cocked, whereupon the reciprocating slide cocks the hammer for the subsequent single-action rounds.

Glock double-action-only pistol with the reciprocating slide locked back.

Finally, "double-action-only" refers to a handgun where the hammer cannot be cocked manually or by the reciprocating slide. Instead, only the trigger cocks and fires the handgun. These guns are designed to prevent accidental or unrecognized cocking of

Chapter Nine

the handgun, and they do not require the user to remember to de-cock when firing is complete.[38]

Revolvers

Revolvers are available in all three action types. Only double-action and double-action-only revolvers should be purchased for defensive use.

Single-action revolvers, which require thumb-cocking before each shot, are **not** recommended for defensive use. These revolvers use the same operating mechanism as cowboy guns and are slow to fire. Even more problematic is their reloading method. While double-action revolvers have swing-out cylinders that allow simultaneous reloading of each chamber, single-action revolvers only reload one cartridge at a time through a small gate. Although they were state-of-the-art in 1870, single-action revolvers are not recommended for defensive use. In contrast, double-action and double-action-only revolvers are very suitable for defensive use.

Revolver proponents cite several advantages of revolvers over pistols: revolvers are simpler to understand and operate; they aren't as dependent on quality ammunition; and they're generally less expensive for the same level of quality. Pistol supporters argue that revolvers generally hold less ammunition, and trigger pulls are frequently heavier than those found on many pistols. All of these arguments have some validity.

---

[38] Functionally, DAO pistols include models that are partially pre-cocked by movement of the slide. Because final cocking is done by the trigger, these guns are functionally classified DAO. These include Safe Action by Glock™, DAK by SigArms™, LEM by H&K™, and Quick Action by Walther™.

Selecting a Defensive Handgun

The simplicity of a revolver is an advantage to people who practice infrequently. A well-known trainer is quoted as saying, "You have to be really stupid to have an accidental discharge with a revolver, but only a little stupid to have one with a semi-automatic pistol."[39] Because all of the cartridges are visible when the cylinder is opened, it's relatively easy to determine whether a double-action revolver is loaded. Furthermore, the defender does not have to remember to deactivate a safety lever before they are able to fire. A simple press of the trigger fires the handgun.

Another advantage of revolvers is their ability to use less powerful ammunition while the defender is learning to shoot. For example, a .357 Magnum revolver is very flexible in ammunition. In addition to being able to use powerful .357 ammunition, it can also chamber and use .38 Special. And .38 ammunition is available in various power ranges such as very light target loads, suitable for initial training, all the way up to relatively heavy self-defense loads. Pistols, on the other hand, generally function well only with full-power ammunition. Firing light loads in a pistol will usually cause stoppages, while light loads in a revolver will function fine.

Because the revolver's trigger cocks the hammer as the gun is fired, trigger pulls of revolvers often weigh eight to twelve pounds. Quality handguns will generally have somewhat lighter trigger pulls, as will those that are adjusted by a gunsmith. As long as the trigger pull is smooth, excellent shooting can be done with a double-action trigger press.

Defensive revolvers should always be fired double-action, and revolvers converted to double-action-only are an excellent idea. Eliminating the

---

[39] The Truth About Self Protection, p. 352

Chapter Nine

single-action capability removes the possibility of a claim that the defender cocked the gun and then accidentally and negligently shot the attacker. (If the defender accidentally shot the attacker, self defense cannot be used as a court defense by the shooter.)

Revolvers are available with barrel lengths varying from two inches to eight inches or more. Common lengths for concealable revolvers are two to four inches. Two-inch revolver barrels are easier to conceal, while four-inch barrels are easier to shoot accurately.

Bianchi "speed-strip," loading the 3rd and 4th of six cartridges.

Revolver grips are interchangeable and inexpensive. Small smooth grips are easier to conceal, while larger rubbery grips might provide recoil absorption and better control. The user should purchase a grip that best meets their particular needs. Be sure, however, that the grips chosen do not interfere with the use of a speedloader, and that they fit the user's hand properly (as described in the "Grip" section of Chapter Two).

Revolver frames are available in steel, aluminum, and ultra-lightweight materials such as scandium or titanium alloys. As the weight of a revolver decreases, its recoil increases. In other words, an otherwise-identical gun with an aluminum frame will recoil harder than the same gun with a steel frame, though the lighter gun will be more convenient to carry.

Selecting a Defensive Handgun

Because revolvers don't use detachable magazines, spare ammunition is best carried in a speedloader. Speedloaders manufactured by HKS or Safariland are recommended. A more compact "speed strip" is manufactured by Bianchi. Although it only allows loading two rounds at a time, it is significantly thinner than a typical speedloader and thus easier to conceal. The least-preferred method is carrying loose rounds. Loose rounds are not organized for quick reloads, and are more likely to be damaged or lost.

Revolver Recommendations

Revolvers manufactured by Smith & Wesson, Colt, Ruger, or Taurus usually serve well. Revolvers should have barrels of two to four inches in length, with steel or aluminum frames. Revolvers with two-inch barrels and aluminum frames are convenient and easy to conceal, but their light weight and short barrels make them difficult to shoot well. Four-inch barrels are more difficult to conceal.

Suitable revolver calibers for concealed carry include .38 Special and .357 Magnum. Revolvers chambered for .357 Magnum are also able to use .38 Special ammunition, although the reverse is *not* true. Calibers smaller than .38 are not recommended. Calibers larger than .357, such as the .41 or .44 Magnum, are more powerful than required and are more difficult to shoot accurately. Some revolvers are chambered for cartridges more commonly used in semi-automatic pistols, such as .45ACP or .40 S&W. While these are serviceable, they are not size-efficient when compared to pistols using the same cartridge.

Chapter Nine

Pistols

As mentioned, the pistol has a few advantages over the revolver, although it suffers drawbacks as well. Although many pistols have lighter trigger pulls than revolvers, no pistol is as flexible in ammunition. Pistols may malfunction if the ammunition is loaded too lightly, the magazine's feed lips are damaged, or the gun is fired with an unlocked wrist. Pistols have more springs to maintain. If the proper unloading procedure is not followed, the user will have a loaded gun he or she believes—incorrectly—to be unloaded. Reliable pistols generally cost more than a reliable revolver, although the pistol holds more ammunition and is generally easier to shoot more accurately because of its lighter trigger pull.

Suitable defensive pistols are available in single-action, double-action, and double-action-only formats. There are advantages and disadvantages to each of these systems.

Single-action pistol with the hammer cocked and the safety on.

All single-action pistols feature a "safety." In one position, the lever prevents the handgun from firing; in the other position the handgun is ready to fire. The user must train and practice sufficiently to automatically release the safety under life-threatening stress, and to re-apply the safety at the end of a defensive encounter, before re-holstering the pistol.

Double-action pistols should be carried with the hammer de-cocked. This results, however, with a long heavy trigger press for the first shot, followed by light single-action pulls for subsequent shots. Some people find the transition between the first and second shots disconcerting.

Selecting a Defensive Handgun

Furthermore, after a stressful incident where the user might have shot an assailant, the defender must remember to de-cock the pistol. Some DA pistols use a combination safety/de-cocker, while others only have a de-cocker.

Double-action-only models are the "revolvers" of pistols, meaning each trigger pull is identical. Few DAO pistols have safeties. The trigger weight of DAO pistols can vary from moderate to heavy, depending on the handgun selected.

Pistol frames are made of steel, aluminum, or polymer (plastic). Polymer frames are not a liability for pistols, as the reciprocating slide rides on steel inserts molded into the plastic. Any of these frame materials are acceptable.

Pistol Recommendations

Pistols manufactured by Glock, Smith & Wesson, Kimber, Springfield Armory, SigArms, Kahr, Ruger, Colt, or Heckler & Koch should serve well. Although some users prefer barrels as long as five inches, many users find barrels of three or four inches serve best. Generally, pistols with shorter barrels are somewhat more likely to malfunction than those with longer barrels.

Suitable calibers include 9mm Luger/Parabellum, .357 Sig, .40 S&W, and .45ACP. The .380ACP is also commonly used, though its

A .25 pistol and .38 revolver. The .25 is smaller but gives up significant power.

Chapter Nine

performance is marginal. Smaller calibers are not recommended, and though other large calibers are available, they do not offer sufficient advantages to outweigh their increased cost.

Maintaining the Handgun

Although many people believe revolvers are less maintenance-intensive than pistols, all handgun types require periodic cleaning and maintenance to ensure reliability. The firearm should be cleaned and lubricated following the directions in the owner's manual. If no owner's manual was included with the handgun, manufacturers will provide one at no charge.

Pistol magazine and recoil springs should be replaced following the manufacturer's suggestions. Magazine lips should be carefully inspected for damage after every practice session. If a specific magazine is identified as causing malfunctions, it should be replaced.

The interior of the barrel, chamber, and magazine must be kept clean and dry. Lubricants can penetrate the seals of the cartridge and cause the primer or powder to fail to ignite.

Handgun Modifications

Contrary to the impression left by most gun magazines, few handguns require extensive modification before they are suitable for defensive use. Indeed, many malfunctions are caused by improper and/or unnecessary modification of handguns that were otherwise reliable.

Revolvers

Revolvers usually do not require any modification for defensive use. If desired, gunsmiths can modify a double-action revolver to double-action-only function at low cost. They can also smooth unusually heavy or gritty trigger pulls for easier function. However, the gunsmith should be informed that reliability and cartridge ignition is most important to the user, and no springs should be lightened. Replacing too-large or too-small grips can be done by the owner without difficulty.

More esoteric modifications could include modification of the cylinder for easier reloads, oversize cylinder latches, aftermarket sights, and a plethora of unnecessary gadgets. Generally these modifications are not necessary—the user will see greater improvement by investing the cost of the modification in additional ammunition for increased practice. Trigger shoes, which clamp to the trigger to make it wider, should be avoided at all costs for reliability reasons.

Pistols

Pistols in factory condition shouldn't require modification to function correctly. If a new pistol won't function reliably after a 200-round break-in period, it should be returned to the factory for adjustment or repair under warranty.

As with revolvers, gunsmiths can smooth unusually heavy or gritty trigger pulls, but a trigger weight of less than four pounds is undesirable. A too-light trigger can be difficult to feel under stress.

Invest in quality magazines, inspect them often, and carefully tend them. Poor or damaged magazines are a frequent cause of reliability issues.

Chapter Nine

The pistol's grip can be modified by changing grip panels (on pistols equipped with them), or the addition of rubber sleeves, to obtain a better fit in the hand.

Pistols that use an external hammer may pinch or "bite" the web of the hand (between thumb and trigger finger). Some users have a "beaver-tail" safety installed to prevent the hammer from contacting the web of the hand. Such installation, if necessary, should be performed by a gunsmith.

Many gunsmiths offer expensive reliability or accuracy packages consisting of "throating," "porting," and/or tightening of the slide-to-frame fit. A reliable handgun doesn't need these modifications.

Selecting Ammunition

At a minimum, the defender should carry one complete reload of the firearm. While the "average" gunfight might only last two or three rounds, this statistic means very little. After all, the "average" attacker breaks off when a defender produces a firearm, without any shots being fired. Is it smart to bet your life on how a criminal assailant—already, by definition, irrational—will behave? Furthermore, multiple assailants might require more than one gun load of ammunition, and malfunction clearing requires the availability of a complete reload to restore the gun's functioning.

Selecting a Defensive Handgun

Defensive Ammunition

Handgun ammunition has improved greatly in the last 20 years, primarily as a result of standards adopted after an F.B.I. shoot-out in Miami. Defensive handgun ammunition should use a "hollow-point" bullet.

These bullets are designed to expand in diameter when they strike a person. This makes the bullet more likely to affect a physiological system that will force the assailant to cease their attack. It has the additional advantage of causing the bullet to rapidly slow down and even stop inside the assailant. This reduces the likelihood of the bullet exiting the attacker's body and striking another person farther downrange.

Ammunition is available in different power levels. "+P" ammunition is loaded to a higher pressure, resulting in higher velocities and higher recoil. In smaller calibers, such as .38 Special and 9mm Parabellum, +P loads might be considered but are not absolutely necessary. In other calibers, +P loads are unnecessary.

An illustration of different bullet types. Three lead semi-wadcutter hollow points, two Speer Gold Dot hollow points, and 1 full-metal-jacket practice round.

For maximum reliability, only ammunition produced by one of the four major, reputable manufacturers should be carried for defensive use. The major manufacturers are Remington, Federal, Winchester, and Speer. Each offers a suitable defensive load in every common caliber. Police departments across the country use these rounds with good reason: these brands are reliable, reputable, and effective. Premier loads

Chapter Nine

suitable for defensive use include Winchester's "Ranger" or "SXT," Federal's "HST," Speer's "Gold Dot," and Remington's "Golden Saber." Most other hollow-point ammunition produced by these manufacturers is also acceptable, though not quite as likely to perform in an ideal fashion as the specified bullet types.

Exotic "pre-fragmented" ammunition also exists, such as Glaser Safety Slugs™ and MagSafe™ cartridges. Ammunition of this type is not recommended. Its penetration is inadequate to guarantee successful physiological effect. Furthermore, its expense precludes most people from firing 200 rounds through their handgun to ensure it functions properly.

Practice Ammunition

Although the defensive ammunition listed above is excellent, most handgun shooters take advantage of economical "practice" loads for their non-defensive shooting. These loads cost less because inexpensive "full-metal-jacketed" or solid lead bullets are used. The extra steps needed to produce a hollow point are left out. The cartridge cases aren't nickel-plated, and the powder is without any flash retardant. While suitable for practice, these loads are unsuitable for defensive use unless nothing else is available.

Every one of the major manufacturers makes these practice loads. In addition, lesser-known manufacturers can be considered for practice ammunition. For example, Black Hills is a reputable company that re-uses fired cases to produce economical practice loads. Some gun stores also sell house brands of remanufactured ammunition, and many hobbyists make their own practice ammunition by refilling the fired case with bulk-purchased components.

Selecting a Defensive Handgun

While "reloaded" ammunition is less expensive, the quality is completely dependent upon the person doing the remanufacturing. The buyer is cautioned to consider the cost/benefit ratio, and *always* wear eye protection. Furthermore, the use of reloaded ammunition voids the manufacturer's warranty for many firearms, and reloaded ammunition, regardless of the quality, should not be used for defensive purposes.

Subcaliber practice

Even less-expensive practice is possible by using kits that convert handguns to use .22 rimfire ammunition. This ammunition is much less powerful—and much less expensive—than even reloaded ammunition, and the cost of the kit can be repaid by one afternoon's extensive practice. Ciener™ and Advantage Arms™ manufacture .22 conversions for various handguns, and .22 revolvers are available that duplicate the size and function of full-caliber revolvers. These are useful training aids that reduce the expense of firing full-power practice loads. They provide the same feel and malfunction drill as their full-power counterparts, and provide the same accuracy. The only component missing is the recoil. Thus, they should not replace the regular firing of the actual defensive handgun, but they can increase the amount of training that can be afforded.

Chapter Nine

Glossary

Action: The operating mechanism of a *pistol* or *revolver*. Action types include "single action," "double action," and "double-action-only," along with trademarked names describing otherwise similar actions.

Barrel: The hollow tube through which the *bullet* travels after it is fired. The barrel is "rifled," meaning it has small lands and grooves that cause the bullet to spin while it moves forward, stabilizing it during flight.

Bullet: The projectile that is launched out of the *barrel*. Before firing it is a component of the *cartridge*. There are different types of bullets, including "hollow point," "full-metal jacket," "wadcutter," etc.

Caliber: The diameter of the interior of the *barrel*, in either inches or millimeters. Sometimes used interchangeably with *cartridge*, as in, "What caliber is your handgun?", even though different *cartridges* may have the same *caliber* (*examples*: .40 S&W and 10mm Auto; .38 Special and .357 Magnum).

Cartridge: A complete piece of ammunition, consisting of the *bullet*, cartridge case, gunpowder, and primer. The trade name of a cartridge describes the *caliber* of the *bullet*. Common cartridges include .22LR, .32ACP, .380ACP, 9mm Luger, .38 Special, .357 Magnum, .357 Sig, .40 S&W, .44 Magnum, and .45ACP.

Chamber: The location of a handgun that contains *cartridges* about to be fired. *Pistols* have one chamber at the beginning of the *barrel*. *Revolvers* have 5-9 chambers in the *cylinder*.

Concealment: An object used to conceal someone's location, although it will not stop *bullets*. Example: darkness, bushes, interior doors.

Cover: An object capable of stopping *bullets*. Examples: concrete walls, thick trees.

Cylinder: In a *revolver*, the revolving portion immediately behind the *barrel*, containing multiple *chambers* where ammunition is held to be rotated in-line with the *barrel* for firing.

Glossary

Dry-Fire: A practice technique used to develop skill, particularly trigger control. The user "fires" the unloaded gun to practice the desired skills. It is vitally important the gun is properly unloaded and separated from ammunition to prevent accidental or negligent firing of the weapon. *Dry-fire* is the opposite of *live-fire*.

Four Stages of Competence: In skill development there are four levels of competence:

1. Unconscious incompetence. The learner cannot perform a skill and is unaware of, or unmotivated, to acquire such a skill.
2. Conscious incompetence. The learner cannot perform the skill, but recognizes their deficit.
3. Conscious competence. The learner can perform a skill while they expend conscious effort to perform it.
4. Unconscious competence. The learner can perform the skill without significant conscious thought.

Frame: The non-moving part of the handgun that includes the grip but not the *slide, cylinder,* or *barrel*.

Line of Attack: The direction in which an attack is committed. By moving off this line, the attack misses the defender and the attacker must re-orient to the defender's position.

Live-fire: The actual firing of a handgun using ammunition, as opposed to *dry-fire* practice where no ammunition is used.

Low Ready: A preparatory position (gun drawn) from which to verbally challenge an assailant when it's not necessary to shoot immediately.

Magazine: The container that stores removable *cartridges* in *pistols* until they are fed into the *chamber*. Spring pressure pushes *cartridges* up into the path of the *slide*.

Pistol: A semi-automatic handgun that stores its ammunition in a removable *magazine* inside the grip. A spring-powered reciprocating *slide* pushes ammunition out of the *magazine* into the *chamber* of the *barrel* for firing.

Glossary

Revolver: A handgun that utilizes a revolving *cylinder* to hold its supply of ammunition. Operation of the trigger or hammer causes the *chambers* to consecutively line up with the *barrel* for firing.

Round: An informal name for *cartridge*.

Semi-automatic: A firearm that uses the energy of the just-fired *cartridge* to operate its *action*, preparing the next *cartridge* for firing. In handguns, this involves the use of a *slide* that is forced backwards in recoil, removing the fired *cartridge* case as it goes backward. During its rearward travel it compresses a recoil spring which then forces the *slide* forward, feeding a new *cartridge* from the *magazine* into the *chamber*.

Slide: The reciprocating part of a *pistol*, located above the *frame*.

Speedloader: A device used to quickly reload a *revolver* with spare *cartridges*. Unlike *magazines*, speedloaders are not an integral part of the firearm and are discarded after the *revolver* is reloaded.

Sweeping: The unsafe act of pointing a weapon at a target the user is not willing to destroy. This is a violation of one of the cardinal rules of firearm safety.

Glossary

Bibliography

Adams, Ronald J. & Thomas McTernan and Charles Remsberg. <u>Street Survival: Tactics for Armed Encounters</u>. Northbrook, Illinois: Calibre Press, 1990.

Artwohl, Dr. Alexis & Loren W. Christensen. <u>Deadly Force Encounters: What Cops Need to Know to Mentally and Physically Prepare for and Survive a Gunfight</u>. Boulder, Colorado: Paladin Press, 1997.

Ayoob, Massad. <u>In the Gravest Extreme: The Role of the Firearm in Personal Protection</u>. Concord, New Hampshire: Police Bookshelf, 1980.

Ayoob, Massad. <u>Stressfire: Vol. I of Gunfighting for Police: Advanced Tactics and Techniques</u>. Concord, New Hampshire: Police Bookshelf, 1992.

Ayoob, Massad. <u>The Truth about Self Protection</u>. New York, New York: Bantam Books, 1991.

Cirillo, Jim. <u>Guns, Bullets, and Gunfights: Lessons and Tales from a Modern-Day Gunfighter</u>. Boulder, Colorado: Paladin Press, 1996.

Crews, Jim. <u>Some of the Answer, Handgun: An Advanced Handgun Technique Manual</u>. Stevensville, Montana: Jim Crews, 2002.

de Becker, Gavin. <u>The Gift of Fear: Survival Signals that Protect Us from Violence</u>. New York, New York: Dell Publishing, 1997.

Farnam, John. <u>The Farnam Method of Defensive Handgunning</u>. Boulder, Colorado: DTI Publications, 2000.

Grossman, Lt. Col. Dave with Loren W. Christensen. <u>On Combat: The Psychology and Physiology of Deadly Conflict in War and in Peace</u>. PPCT Publications, 2004.

Grossman, Lt. Col. Dave. <u>On Killing: The Psychological Cost of Learning to Kill in War and Society</u>. New York: Little, Brown and Company, 1996.

Bibliography

McKee, Tiger. <u>The Book of Two Guns</u>. Langston, AL: Shootrite LLC, 2004.

Morrison, Gregory Boyce. <u>The Modern Technique of the Pistol</u>. Paulden, Arizona: Gunsite Press, 1991.

Mroz, Ralph. <u>Defensive Shooting for Real-Life Encounters: A Critical Look at Current Training Methods</u>. Boulder, Colorado: Paladin Press, 2000.

Quigley, Paxton. <u>Not an Easy Target: Paxton Quigley's Self-Protection for Women</u>. New York, New York: Simon & Schuster, 1995.

Spaulding, Dave. <u>Handgun Combatives</u>. Flushing, New York: Looseleaf Law Publications, 2003.

Stanford, Andy. <u>Fight at Night: Tools, Techniques, Tactics, and Training for Combat in Low Light and Darkness</u>. Boulder, Colorado: Paladin Press, 1999.

Surefire Institute. <u>"Officer Survival in Low Light Conditions" Instructor Handbook</u>. Fountain Valley, California: Surefire Institute, 2001.

U.S. Department of Justice Federal Bureau of Investigation. <u>Law Enforcement Officers Killed and Assaulted</u>. Clarksburg, West Virginia, 1990-2005.

U.S. Department of Justice Federal Bureau of Investigation. <u>In the Line of Fire: Violence Against Law Enforcement</u>. Clarksburg, West Virginia, 1997.

U.S. Department of Justice Federal Bureau of Investigation. <u>Violent Encounters: A Study of Felonious Assaults on Our Nation's Law Enforcement Officers</u>. FBI Publication #0383. Clarksburg, West Virginia, 2006.

Wisconsin Department of Justice Law Enforcement Standards Board. <u>Firearms: A Training Guide for Law Enforcement Officers</u>. Madison, Wisconsin: WI D.O.J., 2002.

Do you have a comment, suggestion, critique, or criticism for the author? Contact me via e-mail: glenn.rehberg@gmail.com

0023932-001

Non Returnable Tinted Color

CAUTION: To assure consistent color always order enough paint to complete the job and intermix all containers of the same color before application. Mixed colors may vary slightly from color strip or color chip.

	ONE GALLON	ULTRADE
	A891001S4	6403923

6166 ECLIPSE
SHER-COLOR FORMULA

BAC COLORANT	OZ	32	64	128
W1-White	2	38	1	-
B1-Black	4	6	-	-
R2-Maroon	-	-	1	1
Y3-Deep Gold	2	49	1	1

SHERWIN-WILLIAMS   09/05
Sher-Color(tm)   Order# 2436-0023
ARCHITECTURAL   IFC 7
EXTERIOR   LA
SUPER PAINT
SATIN

Made in the USA